MW00357052

*The Rational Guide To*

# *Building Small Business Credit*

**PUBLISHED BY**

**Rational Press** - An imprint of the Mann Publishing Group
710 Main Street, 6th Floor
PO Box 580
Rollinsford, NH 03869, USA
www.rationalpress.com
www.mannpublishing.com
+1 (603) 601-0325

Copyright © 2007 by Mann Publishing Group.

All rights reserved. No part of the contents of this book may be reproduced in any form or by any means without the written permission of the publisher. For questions about rights and permissions, send e-mail to permissions@mannpublishing.com.

ISBN-10: 1-932577-34-3
ISBN-13: 978-1-932577-34-1
Library of Congress Control Number (LCCN): 2007921559
Printed and bound in the United States of America.
10  9  8  7  6  5  4  3  2  1

**Trademarks**

Mann Publishing, Mann Publishing Group, Agility Press, Rational Press, Inc.Press, NetImpress, Farmhouse Press, BookMann Press, The Rational Guide To, Rational Guides, ExecuGuide, AdminExpert, From the Source, the Mann Publishing Group logo, the Agility Press logo, the Rational Press logo, the Inc.Press logo, Timely Business Books, Rational Guides for a Fast-Paced World, and Custom Corporate Publications are all trademarks or registered trademarks of Mann Publishing Incorporated.

All brand names, product names, and technologies presented in this book are trademarks or registered trademarks of their respective holders.

**Disclaimer of Warranty**

While the publisher and author(s) have taken care to ensure accuracy of the contents of this book, they make no representation or warranties with respect to the accuracy or completeness of the contents of this book and specifically disclaim any implied warranties or merchantability or fitness for a specific purpose. The advice, strategies, or steps contained herein may not be suitable for your situation. You should consult with a professional where appropriate before utilizing the advice, strategies, or steps contained herein. Neither the publisher nor author(s) shall be liable for any loss of profit or any other commercial damages, including but not limited to special, incidental, consequential, or other damages.

**Credits**

| | |
|---|---|
| Author: | Barbara Weltman |
| Technical Editor: | Louis J. Celli, Jr. |
| Editorial Director: | Jeff Edman |
| Copy Editor: | Kim Turner |
| Artwork: | Scott Gardenhire |
| Indexer: | Christine Frank |
| Series Concept: | Anthony T. Mann |
| Cover Concept: | Marcelo Paiva |

All Mann Publishing Group books may be purchased at bulk discounts.

Rational Press is not affiliated with IBM Corporation or Rational Software.

The Rational Guide To

# Building Small Business Credit

Barbara Weltman

*Foreword by Vicki Raeburn, Chief Quality Officer, D&B*

RATIONAL
PRESS

An imprint of the
www.mannpublishing.com

# About the Author

Barbara Weltman is the nation's leading authority on small business. She has written several top-selling books, including *J.K. Lasser's Small Business Taxes*, *The Complete Idiot's Guide to Starting an eBay® Business,* and she co-authored the *Small Business Survival Book*. She is a respected columnist for Inc.com, Staples.com, and *Bottomline/Personal*, and a contributing writer for *PINK* magazine. Barbara is a sought-after media commentator and has been featured in the *New York Times*, *Wall Street Journal*, *Washington Post*, Forbes.com, Marketwatch.com, *Fox News*, *CNNRadio*, and *CNBC*.

Barbara also edits and publishes *Barbara Weltman's Big Ideas for Small Business*®, a free monthly online newsletter addressing the unique needs and interests of the small business community, and Small Business Idea of the Day, a daily e-mail tip for entrepreneurs, at www.barbaraweltman.com.

Barbara can be reached at info@barbaraweltman.com.

# Acknowledgements

A number of people generously helped educate me on specific topics included in this book and they deserve thanks. They include Jerry Silberman of Commerical Credit Counseling, Paramus, NJ; Edward Mendlowitz, CPA of WithumSmith+Brown, New Brunswick, NJ; and Ross Mazer of Chase, White Plains, NY.

I would also like to acknowledge publisher Tony Mann, who came up with the topic and tirelessly encouraged me to bring this to fruition.

*Rational Guides for a*
*Fast-Paced World* ™

# About Rational Guides

Rational Guides, from Rational Press, provide a no-nonsense approach to publishing based on both a practicality and price that make them rational. Each Rational Guide is constructed with the highest quality writing and production materials—at an affordable price. All Rational Guides are intended to be as complete as possible in a compact size. Furthermore, all Rational Guides come with bonus materials, such as additional chapters, applications, code, utilities, or other resources. To download these materials, just register your book at www. rationalpress.com. See the instruction page at the end of this book to find out how to register your book.

# Who Should Read This Book

This book is intended for small-business owners looking to grow their companies. It can't be done without credit, and this book has been written to provide guidance on how to obtain it. You'll find step-by-step instructions on how to create and protect a business credit profile. Whether you are just starting out, recovering from financial difficulties, or wanting to better understand the role that business credit plays in running a business, *The Rational Guide To Building Small Business Credit* is for you.

# Foreword

*By Vicki Raeburn, Chief Quality Officer, D&B*

It has frequently been said that a significant component of the growth of the U.S. economy is fueled by the creation and ongoing success of small businesses. At D&B, we know that the success of small businesses is a function of many things. We also know that the successful creation of credit by small business has a significant effect on one of the most important business drivers, namely cash flow.

Let's take just a moment to put small business into context. The Internal Revenue Service estimated that there were 30 million businesses filing tax returns in 2005. D&B estimates that more than 75% of the businesses filing returns had taxable revenues of less than $100,000. And, more than 90% of the businesses filing returns had less than $500,000 in revenues. Small businesses, in short, are a very significant part of the economy.

At D&B, we also know that the first few years of running a small business are the hardest. When we talk about small businesses, we differentiate between "start-ups" and "survivors." Start-ups are generally less than two years old. They are struggling to establish their product line, find appropriate office or retail space, attract customers and establish relationships with suppliers and vendors. Start-ups also tend to be volatile because they must be opportunistic to survive the first few years. They need business credit, but they haven't been around long enough to create a full credit profile.

Survivors, on the other hand, have already achieved a level of stability. However, they may only be doing business with other small businesses and their credit profile may be incomplete. That said, both survivors and start-ups need to realize the importance of building their business credit, so that they can maintain it over time and learn how to evaluate the creditworthiness of their suppliers and customers—now and in the future.

*The Rational Guide To Building Small Business Credit* will equip both survivors and start-ups with the information needed to understand and build business credit. Barbara Weltman has put together an insightful reference book that covers the entire gamut of critical issues and questions often left unaddressed. And she has done so at a time when several trends make establishing a strong business credit profile particularly important.

First, many banks, credit card issuers, leasing companies, etc., are automating their credit decisions. This means that any given small business relationship with the bank or the leasing company is much less important than the information in their credit report. The credit report alone will determine small businesses' credit limit and the interest rate that they will pay. This holds true also for insurance policy rates, the payment terms set by suppliers, and even rents—all of which may be determined by the quality of a small business's credit. As interest rates return to normal levels, these credit decisions will have a significant effect on their cash flow. Building a good small business credit report can help transform any entrepreneur from being a "start-up" to achieving the small business "survivor" status.

In light of these trends, Barbara Weltman's contribution is very timely and relevant. Thoughtfully divided into four sections, *The Rational Guide To Building Small Business Credit* will take the reader through the beginner's basics to steps small businesses can take to improve their credit. The sections covering "Advanced Concepts" and bonus resources will give readers the keys to mastering the subject of commercial credit.

I am confident that this book will encourage small business owners and entrepreneurs to manage their business credit as carefully as their personal credit. I hope that small businesses will learn some very valuable lessons through this resource. Once you have a clearer understanding of the importance of managing business credit, you will be that much further along the path to achieving small business success.

# Introduction

The ability to access capital—being able to borrow money or buy on credit at reasonable interest rates—is vital to the health and success of your company. Having insufficient capital is often identified as a top reason why businesses fail. While it is difficult to substantiate this claim, it is certain that businesses need sufficient money to exist.

Unfortunately, small businesses face a catch-22 when it comes to their access to money. They need capital to start up, operate, and grow. But the very nature of being a small business makes it a challenge to access this needed capital. Small businesses usually lack the financial resources that would diminish their credit risk. They operate on thin margins and are vulnerable to shifting market conditions, and this tends to turn off the money spigots of commercial lenders.

The reality is that most small businesses must borrow money from time to time. There's no good way around this fact, so small businesses, which face greater obstacles when seeking capital, are often forced to seek alternative ways to raise the funds they need.

Funding can be obtained by seeking *equity financing* from additional investors, but this usually isn't a good solution for entrepreneurs. Equity financing means sharing the profits with investors and, in many cases, also involves sharing the glory for accomplishments and ceding some decision-making authority.

Alternatively, funding needs can be met by "creative" borrowing. Lenders may finance loans by using your accounts receivables (factoring) or even credit card receipts. These and other borrowing alternatives may get you the money you need, but you'll pay a high price—higher than a commercial loan. It is not uncommon to wind up paying usurious rates for the money you use. Some states fix a limit on the rate interest that can be charged. For example, a lender cannot charge a business more than 5% over the Federal Reserve

Bank of San Francisco's interest rate. The District of Columbia imposes a flat 24% rate limit on loans. New Jersey's rates are capped at 30% for noncorporate borrowers and 50% for corporate borrowers. There are other states, such as South Dakota and Virginia, that have no usury rate—the sky's the limit (Wisconsin has no limit on rates charged to corporate borrowers).

Many small businesses may be under some misconceptions when it comes to SBA loans. The U.S. Small Business Administration (SBA) does *not* make loans. Rather, it provides certain loan guarantees to lenders as a way to induce them to make loans to small businesses. It also supports programs (loans from certain non-profit organizations) for small-business lending. For example, under the 7(a) loan program, one of the SBA's main lending programs for borrowing up to $2 million, the government guarantees the loan up to $1 million. The commercial lender is only on the hook for half the principal.

There are only a handful of ways in which a small business can gain easier access to capital. This book is here to help you establish business credit so that the avenues of capital remain open to your business. From an owner's perspective, it's important for a company to have its own credit, separate and apart from that of the owner. Business credit will enable businesses to obtain financing more easily and commend their borrowing on a more favorable basis. With proper guidance, this is something that every business can strive to achieve.

The importance of a small business's credit is a relatively new and evolving area; in the past, focus was placed on the owner's personal credit as a means of financing. Thus, the information and assistance available to small-business owners seeking company credit is limited. This book helps to fill the void and offers a valuable resource for entrepreneurs in today's marketplace.

The book is divided into three parts:

- ◆ Part I covers credit fundamentals — why borrowing is essential to business, the importance of business credit, and resources for finding money you need on a credit basis.

- ◆ Part II discusses the basics of credit building for your business — how to use credit cards to build business credit, using vendor financing to build up credit, applying for a secured bank loan, and working with Dun & Bradstreet to build up your company's credit.

- Part III covers more advanced concepts of credit — monitoring and protecting your credit profile, re-establishing credit after serious financial problems, working with the government on a basis that involves your credit, and finally, running a credit check on those with whom you do business.

Hopefully, business owners will devote the time and attention they should to understanding the business credit process, so they can position their company to borrow money when they need it.

# Contents

# Contents

# Contents

# Credit Fundamentals

# Chapter 1

# Business Borrowing is Vital

Benjamin Franklin said "If you would like to know the value of money, go and try to borrow some." For small businesses, this is a hard lesson to learn. Nonetheless, borrowing is an integral part of running a company, and every business owner must master this lesson to learn how to borrow better.

Your word may be your bond, but a good business credit rating is essential to borrowing money on favorable terms. Merely promising to repay a loan won't get you the funds you want. Commercial lenders will look to objective standards to assess whether to advance money to your company.

This chapter explains why you may need to borrow money as your company evolves. It discusses the Five C's of credit analysis, which are used by commercial lenders to assess your creditworthiness. Finally, this chapter puts small-business borrowing in perspective by contrasting the borrowing opportunities open to larger companies with the obstacles facing smaller ones. Later chapters discuss other borrowing options, such as obtaining terms from vendors with whom you do business.

## Why Borrow Money?

Unless you are a trust fund baby or just won the lottery, you probably need to look beyond your piggy bank to finance business start-up and expansion.

You could wait to amass, via savings, all of the funds you'll require for the growth of your business, but this will significantly stall your business plans. For example, it would take you nearly seven years to accumulate $100,000 if you put $1,000 each month in a savings account earning 5% interest (This is regardless of the taxes that could further delay achieving your savings goal).

You could bring in investors to become partners in your business. This option may be desirable when an investor brings more than just money to the table, such as skills, connections, or attributes that could be advantageous to the future of your business. However, bringing in additional owners is probably not desirable when money is the only benefit to the deal. This dilutes your ownership interest and often means that they have some say in the operations of the company for as long as they continue to have an ownership interest.

You can grow your business much faster and with greater control if you don't wait to build savings or take in new partners. There are a number of good reasons why it makes sense to borrow money now, including:

▶ **Acquiring assets** — This means buying equipment or real property for your company. Your business may need certain equipment to operate effectively. Instead of leasing the items you need, you can purchase them. In certain situations, it's an alternative that makes sense (e.g., where you intend to retain assets beyond the normal lease period). You may otherwise have an opportunity to buy the facilities you operate from—an office, medical building, storefront, factory or warehouse. To complete the purchase of equipment or real property, you usually need outside financing.

▶ **Replacing outstanding financing** — You may have outstanding debt with terms less favorable than you can obtain today. Replacing outstanding financing means using new low-interest financing to replace existing high-interest loans. For example, you may have obtained a loan when you were just starting up the business and lacked business credit. Today, you have built up an impressive credit profile for your company that can command more favorable loan terms. Old loans may tie up collateral, have a high interest rate, or other terms you would not face on new debt that you can obtain from a different lender.

▶ **Acquiring equity** — In a multi-owner company, when one owner retires or dies, remaining owners usually want to acquire the departing owner's share. Depending on the size of this ownership interest ("equity"), you may need commercial financing to swing the purchase.

▶ **Working capital** — This means paying bills and meeting regular obligations. The need for outside funding for this purpose may arise during seasonal downturns, special circumstances (e.g., an uninsured catastrophic loss) or cash flow challenges (e.g., expectations of revenue that are slow in being paid to you).

# The Five C's of Credit Analysis

Lenders want to lend out their money; it's the way in which they make more money. But they only want to lend it to a borrower who can repay the funds in full and on time.

When small businesses seek commercial financing over certain limits, lenders traditionally rely on the Five C's of credit analysis—*capacity, capital, collateral, conditions*, and *character*—to determine whether the borrower is a good risk. Each C is taken into account; none of these criteria alone will necessarily ensure or prevent your access to funding. There is no magic formula or fixed percentage lenders use to weight each of the Five C's. They are merely factors that lenders use to get a feel for whether a borrower is a good risk for the lending institution.

**Caution:**

When applying for a small loan for $50,000 ("small" is relative to each lender), qualification depends purely on your business and personal credit scores. Lenders don't perform a credit analysis; dependent upon those two scores, they respond either yes or no.

How do you think you stack up? Consider each of the following C's:

▶ **Capacity** — This is an assessment of your ability to repay the funds. The lender wants a good idea of how you plan to repay the money before it will agree to lend it to you. Capacity is determined by several factors, including:

● *Cash flow* refers to the money coming into a company minus the funds going out, measured during a defined period of time. For instance, if you have regular monthly revenue of $10,000 and expenses of $8,000, you have a solid cash flow each month of $2,000 that could be used to service debt. If a company's expenses equal or exceed its revenue, how can it expect to pay back a loan?

- *Payment history* is how timely (or late) your company has been on repaying prior loans. In the past it was more complicated for commercial lenders to determine whether a small business had a good payment history, but today there are credit rating companies, such as Dun & Bradstreet (D&B), that can provide this information to lenders.

- *Contingent sources for repayment* are other resources you have to make good on a loan. These include your personal assets, bank accounts, and other resources at your disposal.

Capacity is the main criterion for lending. A bank or other lender wants to be repaid in the easiest way possible—regular payments from a business's cash flow.

▶ **Capital** — Usually, an owner must have his or her own funds at risk in the company before a commercial lender will pony up. Capital is your investment in your company—what you have at stake and could lose in the event of a company failure. There isn't a fixed percentage or dollar amount that an owner must have at risk before getting a commercial loan. However, most lenders would agree that at least 25% of the money for the company must come from the owner's pocket.

▶ **Collateral** — Solid assets that the lender can sell (if you fail to make payments on your loan), such as heavy machinery or stocks and bonds, can be used as collateral. Unfortunately, lenders do not consider assets such as computers, telephone equipment, and office furniture as property that can be used as collateral. Thus, in the case of most small businesses, the owner's personal assets, including his or her home, are collateral for a company loan. When a small-business owner gives his or her personal guarantee on a loan to the company, the owner promises to use personal assets to satisfy the loan if the company cannot repay the amount borrowed.

▶ **Conditions** — This is a comprehensive assessment of the circumstances surrounding the loan—general economic conditions at the time of the request and the purpose of the loan. Market conditions, including the climate for your industry and the state of the economy as a whole, can factor greatly into a lending decision. Obviously, if you are in a booming industry during a solid economy, it is more likely that a loan will be made than if your industry is dying and the economy is shaky. The purpose of the loan may be considered favorable where funds are used to acquire assets or equity, or less favorable where the funds are used for riskier activities (e.g., expansion into new markets). Most lenders restrict their funding to companies that plan to use the money *only* to increase sales or decrease costs.

▶ **Character** — This highly subjective factor is all about your personal background and your ability to impress the lender as a dependable person who can assure that the company repays its loan. The lender will consider your education, work experience, and personal credit history.

### Note

When looking for a commercial loan, don't forget the importance of personal touch. Work with a bank where you already have a business relationship. Meet with a bank's lending officer (not the bank manager who handles your checking account problems).

# How Small and Mid-Sized Businesses Borrow Money

When it comes to accessing capital, size matters. Large corporations can raise money in a variety of ways that are not open to small businesses, including:

▶ **Public offerings** — Corporations that are public companies can raise money by selling stock or making a bond offering to the public.

▶ **Access to commercial funding** — Most commercial banks are more inclined to make loans to large corporations than to small businesses. The reason is that the loan process is just about the same from the lender's perspective regardless of the size of the loan. It is more profitable for a lender to make larger loans than smaller ones. Because they are at the top of the lending ladder, large corporations continue to have access to capital when the economy is uncertain and lending slows down or dries up. Small businesses may be shut out of the lending market while large corporations continue to be able to borrow.

▶ **Favorable commercial lending terms** — Large corporations typically qualify for the most favorable interest rates available. For example, according to the most recent statistics from the U.S. Small Business Administration (SBA), while large corporate borrowers with minimum risk paid only 5.5% interest on a fixed rate loan taken out in November 2003, small borrowers (with loans under $100,000, called *microloans*) paid 6.53%.

In contrast to large corporations, small and mid-sized businesses have a tougher time obtaining commercial financing. Access to small loans (under $1 million) and microloans (under $100,000) has been declining in recent years while the number and dollars lent for larger loans continued to grow, according to a November 2005 report from the Office of Advocacy of the SBA.

Because of their difficulties obtaining traditional bank loans, small businesses often seek out alternative (more costly) financing options. Instead of a commercial loan, for example, they may rely on credit card borrowing, use finance company loans (which are more costly than bank loans), or seek loans from private lenders, such as "angels" (wealthy individuals who may lend funds or make equity investments in companies because of the opportunity for greater returns on their money than could be obtained through traditional investments).

But small companies do not have to rely on costly financing options; they can build up creditworthiness independent of their owners and enjoy greater access to capital. Turn to the next chapter to see the importance of business credit.

# *Summary*

Whatever stage your business is in—from start-up to growth to maturity—there are many valid reasons for your business to borrow money. The funds you borrow can help you achieve your business objectives efficiently.

Your ability to borrow money on reasonable repayment terms depends on many factors. Lenders will review these factors in making a decision on how much to lend you, and on what terms.

It is important to recognize the distinctions in access to capital between large corporations and small to mid-sized businesses. Large corporations find money more easily, command lower interest rates than small businesses, and have ways to raise funds that are not open to small businesses.

*"I'm sorry, I just think I need to see other banks."*

# Did you know?

One of the biggest mistakes that start-up owners make is asking a bank for 100% of the financing needed to open their doors. Lenders want to see that owners have a personal stake in their business, so be prepared to ante up 30% to 50% of the money to get started.

# Chapter 2

# Business Credit is Better than Personal Credit

One of the risks that a business owner faces is laying his or her personal assets on the line. A house, car, and bank account can be vulnerable to creditors' claims if the business does not borrow wisely.

You may believe that if you own a corporation or a limited liability company (LLC) your personal assets are safe. In theory this is true, because most creditors can look only to the assets of the corporation or LLC to satisfy their claims if the business entity is legitimate (it is not a mere façade that would allow creditors to "pierce the corporate value" to reach owners). For example, if your corporation or LLC loses a lawsuit, only company assets are used to pay the judgment.

However, in practice, you can remain vulnerable. Lenders often require owners to give their personal guarantee for money loaned to the business. If the business fails to repay the loan, the lender can look to the owner's personal assets for satisfaction. Thus, the corporate or LLC entity may protect an owner from lawsuits by injured customers or other disgruntled parties, but it will not, in most cases, shield personal assets in the case of company borrowing where there is an owner's personal guarantee.

Personal exposure is not mandatory. If the business has its own credit history or can establish a credit history, borrowing may be independent of the owner's credit rating. This chapter tells you why business credit is so important. It helps you understand how both personal and business credit is rated and explains the technicalities of the credit rating process.

# How Personal Credit is Rated

Investors may say that past performance is no guarantee of future results, but don't be fooled. Lenders look precisely at past performance—your credit rating—to determine whether you can be expected to pay back a new loan in full and on time. Your credit rating, which is a measure of your creditworthiness, helps lenders determine how reliable you will be in repaying new borrowing.

Lenders use your personal ("consumer") credit rating to determine whether to give you a personal loan—for your home, a car, or other purposes—and how much interest to charge you for borrowing this money. For example, if you wanted to borrow money to purchase a home, you might pay between 5.9% and 7.5% interest for the same loan, depending on your credit rating. Someone with good credit would only pay 5.9%, while someone perceived as a riskier borrower would pay 7.5%. Depending on the size of the loan, this interest rate differential could cost you hundreds of dollars more each month that would have to be paid to the bank. As your credit rating improves, it becomes easier to obtain financing, and you'll pay lower interest rates.

Lenders also use personal credit scores to determine whether to make loans to small businesses. Many types of loans cannot be obtained without the personal guarantee of the owner or owners, even if the business itself has excellent credit. Usually, all owners with an interest of 20% or more must give their personal guarantee; thus, owners need to mind their personal credit as well as their business credit.

A personal credit rating is based on an objective standard fixed by the three major credit rating bureaus: Equifax, Experian, and TransUnion. Each bureau fixes its own score and lenders then average these scores to decide whether and what to lend you. The most common rating system is called FICO®; there is also a new rating system called VantageScore^SM.

## FICO® Score

This rating system looks at various factors and assigns a number, or score, to each one. Not all factors carry the same weight, and both positive and negative factors come into play. Here is a breakdown of the five factors used in your FICO score:

▶ **Payment history (35%)** — Information about how you've managed your money in the past. This includes the number of past due items and how long they've been delinquent. It also examines how long it's been since these items have arisen as well as any collection activities you've experienced. Public records on bankruptcies, judgments, lawsuits, liens, and wage attachments are taken into account.

▶ **Amount owed (30%)** — The total of your outstanding accounts, including the number of balances and the amount owed on each one, greatly affects your FICO score. Credit rating bureaus also look at the proportion of the credit lines you have available to what you've actually used.

▶ **Length of credit history (15%)** — Each of your accounts is separately reviewed to see how long it's been opened and what type of activity has been generated.

▶ **New credit (10%)** —Accounts you've recently established as well as credit inquiries from other lenders are all considered in determining your score.

▶ **Types of credit used (10%)** — This is the number of each type of borrowing, including credit cards and retail accounts.

Not every aspect of your personal life is taken into account when fixing your FICO score. Several personal factors—age, race, color, religion, national origin, sex, and marital status—do not affect the score. Similarly, employment history, current position, compensation, and assets (including ownership in a business) are *not* part of your FICO score. They are, however, separately factored in by lenders when deciding whether to loan you money.

A FICO score ranges from 300 to 900. The best borrowers have a rating of 750 or higher. You can obtain a loan with a score of 650, but you'll pay more interest than you would if your score were higher. The score changes monthly and may rise or fall with changes affecting the rating. For example, paying down a loan balance may boost your score, while falling behind on a payment may reduce your score. A judgment or bankruptcy notation will reduce your score. Applying for a new credit card may reduce your score, though not by much, because of the inquiry about your credit. You can estimate your FICO score using a quick self-test from BankRate.com (www.bankrate.com/brm/fico/calc.asp).

## Keeping Tabs on Your FICO Score

It is highly advisable to watch your FICO score on a regular basis. This will allow you to detect problems and correct them promptly. Problems may be minor (someone else's delinquent payment is included in your report) or severe (identity thieves could use your credit to run up unpaid bills in your name).

*this doesn't include FICO score*

Under federal law you are entitled to a personal annual credit report for free. This will show you everything reported to credit bureaus under your name and Social Security number. To obtain your free report, go to AnnualCreditReport.com (https://www. annualcreditreport.com/cra/index.jsp). If you request your report online through a secure Web site, you obtain the information immediately. You can call a toll-free telephone number to request a report by mail, which takes about two weeks.

To monitor your report more closely, consider using a commercial monitoring service for your FICO score. One example, ScoreWatch™, from Equifax, lets you keep watch over your consumer credit and notifies you when a change to your FICO score is made that impacts your borrowing ability. The annual cost is $79.95.

> ### ✔ Note:
> Monitoring your FICO score is a good way to detect identity theft. If there is a change in your score that you cannot understand or explain, it might be due to someone else obtaining credit under your name and Social Security number.

## VantageScore

The three major consumer credit reporting bureaus—Equifax, Experian, and TransUnion—have teamed up to create a new rating system intended to simplify the credit process for both borrowers and lenders. Supposedly, it uses a more objective methodology to establish a score. It is the first tri-bureau system of its kind.

The VantageScore, which first came into effect in mid-March 2006, has a rating that ranges from 501 to 990. The higher your score is, the better your credit risk becomes. Because it is so new, it is too early to say whether it will gain widespread use by lenders.

**Note:**

To learn more about VantageScore, go to www.equifax.com/vantagescore/index.html.

# Why Rely on Business Credit?

Rather than jeopardize your personal assets every time your business needs money, you may be able to use the company's credit rating to obtain the funds you need on more favorable terms and with much lower interest rates. For example, a business could obtain a 10-year loan for $100,000 at 7% where you would pay 13% for the same amount. With business credit, you could save almost $40,000!

**Caution:**

No matter how good your business credit rating, many lenders continue to require an owner's personal guarantee.

Establishing business credit has greater significance for your company than merely improving its borrowing ability. Business credit is also used by vendors to determine whether to do business with you; having good business credit will facilitate transactions with other companies. A good credit report can also affect your insurance coverage. Before writing new policies, insurers increasingly check company credit ratings.

# How Business Credit is Rated

Like your personal credit rating, each business has or can develop a credit rating on which lenders will base new credit opportunities. When it comes to business credit ratings, Dun and Bradstreet (D&B) (http://smallbusiness.dnb.com) virtually has a lock on the market. D&B has developed a number of ratings tools that companies use to decide whether to do business with you and that lenders use to fix loan terms. Several other companies that offer business credit ratings of their own are briefly introduced at the end of the chapter.

Business credit rating differs in certain respects from a personal credit rating. Unlike personal credit, there is no single or fixed standard for determining business credit, although there is a growing reliance on D&B's PAYDEX—as explained later in this chapter. Unlike a personal FICO score that is based solely on credit history—what you borrow and how you repay your obligations—business ratings are more broadly based, taking into account company size in terms of assets and employees. Unlike personal credit ratings based on information supplied by credit card companies, large retailers, and financial institutions, business credit ratings are created primarily by information supplied by you and gathered from inquiries of your suppliers, vendors, and other trade accounts. Lenders may place greater emphasis on certain elements of the business credit report than others to determine your company's creditworthiness.

A business credit rating is generally separate from an owner's personal credit rating. An owner's poor personal credit is not reflected on a company credit report (although business credit is no substitute for maintaining good personal credit). However, personal and business credit are often commingled when the business is a sole proprietorship or even a limited liability company.

# Understanding the Business Credit Report and its Terminology

When establishing credit for your company or reading a report about companies you may do business with—both customers and vendors—it's important to understand the unique language involved. The following are brief definitions of terms and concepts that will be more fully developed throughout this chapter.

▶ **Average high credit/highest credit** — D&B's levels, based on company's PAYDEX comparison with the industry as a whole; puts credit in perspective.

▶ **Business in good standing** — There are no problems to report.

▶ **Commercial credit score** — D&B determines the likelihood of an account becoming severely delinquent within 12 months.

▶ **Comprehensive report** — This is an amalgam of several D&B reports put together to create a complete picture of a company. It includes PAYDEX, credit score class, and financial stress class, as well as information on public filings (e.g., liens) and history and operations of the business (e.g., when it filed for incorporation, annual financial statement, number of employees, facilities, and affiliate companies).

▶ **Credit score class** — This D&B rating assesses payment habits to provide a likelihood that an account will become delinquent within 12 months. The classes range from 1 to 5, with 1 representing the lowest risk.

▶ **Financial stress score** — This D&B rating predicts the probability of business failure within the coming 12 months, based on the financial stresses that a business is under.

▶ **PAYDEX** — This is D&B's leading payment predictor that you can use to determine whether someone can be expected to pay you on time.

# D&B Ratings

D&B is the premier business credit rating service. Originally, D&B established credit reports and background information primarily on large companies. Information was only available at that time on big corporations that dealt with other large businesses and reported information about them to D&B.

Today, D&B has moved into business credit reporting for small and mid-sized businesses. It has done so in recognition of the need for these companies to have credit separate and apart from their owners in order to prosper.

## D&B Rating Interpretation

This is a rating system measuring the financial strength of a company, based on its net worth or equity (as computed by D&B). The ratings, shown in Table 2.1, range from 5A for large corporations to HH for very small businesses. The ratings are assigned on the basis of financial information that you supply (e.g., your company's financial statement). Then a credit appraisal is assigned for your classification, with "1" being high, "2" good, and "3" fair. Your financial strength is based solely on company size; your composite credit appraisal can vary, depending on your company's credit behavior. For example, a company may be ranked as 1A because its net worth is $600,000, but its composite credit appraisal can be 1, 2, or 3.

| Financial strength | | Composite credit appraisal | | |
|---|---|---|---|---|
| Rating | Assets | High | Good | Fair |
| 5A | $50 million and over | 1 | 2 | 3 |
| 4A | $10 million to $49,999,999 | 1 | 2 | 3 |
| 3A | $1 million to $9,999,999 | 1 | 2 | 3 |
| 2A | $750,000 to $999,999 | 1 | 2 | 3 |
| 1A | $500,000 to $749,999 | 1 | 2 | 3 |
| BA | $300,000 to $499,999 | 1 | 2 | 3 |
| BB | $200,000 to $299,999 | 1 | 2 | 3 |
| CB | $125,000 to $199,999 | 1 | 2 | 3 |
| CC | $75,000 to $124,999 | 1 | 2 | 3 |
| DC | $50,000 to $74,999 | 1 | 2 | 3 |
| DD | $35,000 to $49,999 | 1 | 2 | 3 |
| EE | $20,000 to $34,999 | 1 | 2 | 3 |
| FF | $10,000 to $19,999 | 1 | 2 | 3 |
| GG | $5,000 to $9,999 | 1 | 2 | 3 |
| HH | Up to $4,999 | 1 | 2 | 3 |

**Table 2.1:** 5A to HH Ratings.

The rating classification system is based on the number of employees. There are only two categories: 1R is for companies with 10 or more employees and 2R is for companies with one to nine employees. Again, a composite credit appraisal can be assigned to each class of company.

Table 2.2 outlines the alternative employee range designations, a D&B shorthand description of staff size :

| ER1 | 1000 or more employees |
|-----|------------------------|
| ER2 | 500 to 999 employees |
| ER3 | 100 to 499 employees |
| ER4 | 50 to 99 employees |
| ER5 | 20 to 49 employees |
| ER6 | 10 to 19 employees |
| ER7 | 5 to 9 employees |
| ER8 | 1 to 4 employees |
| ERN | Not available |

**Table 2.2:** Alternative Employee Range Designations.

## D&B PAYDEX

D&B has developed a score interpretation table (see Table 2.3) based on a company's payment habits. More specifically, it is a dollar-weighted measure of a company's payment performance based on the payment experiences for which D&B has information. A higher score indicates that the company is good at paying its bills, and, therefore, their credit risk is better. A score of 80 is perfect—the equivalent of a 750 FICO score for consumers. Most lenders are comfortable with a PAYDEX score of 70.

The score is based on information provided from a company's trade accounts to D&B. You may be asked to supply trade account information (usually a minimum of five trade accounts), so D&B can obtain the necessary data to develop a PAYDEX for your business. The PAYDEX number can be for a 3-month or 12-month period. You can view the trend for this period to see if a company's payment performance is improving or worsening.

PAYDEX is a weighted average; trade accounts reporting higher dollar amounts receive greater importance in scoring than accounts with lower dollar amounts. D&B gives this example: if 10 trades for $50 each report that your company pays 60 days late, but one trade for $10,000 reports that you pay promptly, your score will still be good because the $10,000 trade account outweighs the $50 tardy trades. Of course, this works in reverse, so that one late payment of a sizable trade account means more to your score than 10 timely payments of small trade accounts.

In order to obtain the most favorable credit terms, you want as high a PAYDEX score as possible to show a low risk of late payment. A low risk of late payment is assigned to companies that make their payments promptly (on time) to 30 days within terms. Companies who make payments an average of 30 days beyond terms are given a medium risk of late payment. High risk of late payment is associated with companies who pay an average of 30 to 120 days beyond terms. The PAYDEX value chart showing the PAYDEX score relative to the average number of days it takes to pay what's owed is shown in Table 2.3.

| PAYDEX | Average days to pay |
|--------|---------------------|
| 100 | 30 days sooner than terms |
| 99 | 29 days sooner than terms |
| 98 | 28 days sooner than terms |
| 97 | 27 days sooner than terms |
| 96 | 26 days sooner than terms |
| 95 | 25 days sooner than terms |
| 94 | 24 days sooner than terms |
| 93 | 23 days sooner than terms |
| 92 | 22 days sooner than terms |
| 91 | 21 days sooner than terms |
| 90 | 20 days sooner than terms |
| 89 | 18 days sooner than terms |
| 88 | 16 days sooner than terms |
| 87 | 14 days sooner than terms |
| 86 | 12 days sooner than terms |
| 85 | 10 days sooner than terms |
| 84 | 8 days sooner than terms |
| 83 | 6 days sooner than terms |
| 82 | 4 days sooner than terms |
| 81 | 2 days sooner than terms |
| 80 | On terms |
| 79 | 2 beyond terms |
| 78 | 3 beyond terms |
| 77 | 5 beyond terms |
| 76 | 6 beyond terms |

**Table 2.3:** PAYDEX Value Chart.

| PAYDEX | Average days to pay |
|--------|---------------------|
| 75 | 8 beyond terms |
| 74 | 9 beyond terms |
| 73 | 11 beyond terms |
| 72 | 12 beyond terms |
| 71 | 14 beyond terms |
| 70 | 15 beyond terms |
| 69 | 16 beyond terms |
| 68 | 17 beyond terms |
| 67 | 18 beyond terms |
| 66 | 19 beyond terms |
| 65 | 19 beyond terms |
| 64 | 19 beyond terms |
| 63 | 20 beyond terms |
| 62 | 21 beyond terms |
| 61 | 22 beyond terms |
| 60 | 22 beyond terms |
| 59 | 23 beyond terms |
| 58 | 24 beyond terms |
| 57 | 25 beyond terms |
| 56 | 26 beyond terms |
| 55 | 26 beyond terms |
| 54 | 27 beyond terms |
| 43 | 28 beyond terms |
| 52 | 29 beyond terms |
| 51 | 29 beyond terms |
| 50 | 30 beyond terms |
| 49 | 33 beyond terms |
| 48 | 36 beyond terms |
| 47 | 39 beyond terms |
| 46 | 42 beyond terms |
| 45 | 45 beyond terms |

**Table 2.3:** PAYDEX Value Chart (continued).

| PAYDEX | Average days to pay |
|--------|---------------------|
| 44 | 48 beyond terms |
| 43 | 51 beyond terms |
| 42 | 54 beyond terms |
| 41 | 57 beyond terms |
| 40 | 60 beyond terms |
| 39 | 63 beyond terms |
| 38 | 66 beyond terms |
| 37 | 69 beyond terms |
| 36 | 72 beyond terms |
| 35 | 75 beyond terms |
| 34 | 78 beyond terms |
| 33 | 81 beyond terms |
| 32 | 84 beyond terms |
| 31 | 87 beyond terms |
| 30 | 90 beyond terms |
| 29 | 93 beyond terms |
| 28 | 96 beyond terms |
| 27 | 99 beyond terms |
| 26 | 102 beyond terms |
| 25 | 105 beyond terms |
| 24 | 108 beyond terms |
| 23 | 111 beyond terms |
| 22 | 114 beyond terms |
| 21 | 117 beyond terms |
| 20 | 120 beyond terms |
| 1 to 19 | Over 120 days beyond terms |

**Table 2.3:** PAYDEX Value Chart (continued).

## *Financial Stress Score*

What is the likelihood that a company will stop doing business before paying all its creditors in full within the coming year? This statistical model was developed to predict that very situation. Financial stress classes range from 1 to 5 (see Table 2.4). Businesses that are less likely to leave their creditors high and dry are assigned to the lower financial stress classes. The national average for all U.S. companies in D&B's files is 1.4%. A company with a score of 4 has a moderate to high risk of severe financial stress over the next 12 months. A company that is in bankruptcy or out of business at its current location may have a "0" financial stress class.

D&B also provides the average stress score for companies within the same industry, with the same number of years in business, and the same number of employees within the region in which they operate. This is useful because it can mean that a particular company shares the same financial stresses of all companies within a particular industry, or in a particular area of the country.

| Financial stress class | Financial stress score range | Percentile score range | Incidence of financial stress |
|---|---|---|---|
| 1 | 1377-1875 | 21-100 | 0.49% |
| 2 | 1353-1376 | 11-20 | 1.37% |
| 3 | 1303-1352 | 5-10 | 3.73% |
| 4 | 1225-1302 | 2-4 | 8.30% |
| 5 | 1001-1224 | 1 | 35.80% |

**Table 2.4:** Financial Stress Classes.

## *Commercial Credit*

The commercial credit score is another statistical model D&B uses to predict the likelihood of a company being delinquent in paying a bill during the next 12 months. The score ranges from 101 to 670; each 40 point increase or decrease doubles or halves the risk. For example, a company with a credit score of 460 is twice as likely to become delinquent as one with a score of 500.

The higher the credit score class, which ranges from 1 to 5, the more likely a delinquency. In effect, a score of 5 indicates a company with a poor credit risk because of the high likelihood of delinquency. Delinquency in this instance is defined as payment 90 days or later than the terms of payment required. Table 2.5 defines the five credit score classes. Companies that are in bankruptcy or out of business at their current location may have a "0," which can also denote higher risk situations.

| Credit score class | Commercial credit score range | Credit score percentile | Incidence of delinquency |
|---|---|---|---|
| 1 | 536-670 | 91-100 | 2.5% |
| 2 | 493-535 | 71-90 | 4.8% |
| 3 | 423-492 | 31-70 | 12.9% |
| 4 | 376-422 | 11-30 | 24.2% |
| 5 | 101-375 | 1-10 | 58.8% |

**Table 2.5:** Credit Score Classes.

A company can be assigned a score from the incidence of delinquent payment assignment table (see Table 2.6). The national average is 17.3%, indicating a score between about 36 and 45.

| Minimum score | Maximum score | Incidence of delinquent payment |
|---|---|---|
| 96 | 100 | 2.1% |
| 91 | 95 | 2.9% |
| 86 | 90 | 3.6% |
| 81 | 85 | 4.4% |
| 76 | 80 | 5.2% |
| 71 | 75 | 6.1% |
| 66 | 70 | 7.3% |
| 61 | 65 | 8.7% |
| 56 | 60 | 10.5% |
| 51 | 55 | 12.2% |
| 46 | 50 | 13.9% |
| 41 | 45 | 15.5% |
| 36 | 40 | 17.2% |
| 31 | 35 | 18.4% |
| 26 | 30 | 20.2% |

**Table 2.6:** Incidence of Delinquent Payment Assignments.

| Minimum score | Maximum score | Incidence of delinquent payment |
|---|---|---|
| 21 | 25 | 22.5% |
| 16 | 20 | 24.6% |
| 11 | 15 | 29.6% |
| 6 | 10 | 44.9% |
| 1 | 5 | 72.7% |

**Table 2.6:** Incidence of Delinquent Payment Assignments (continued).

# Other Business Ratings

While D&B is the primary rating company, a number of other companies are getting into this arena to provide small-business solutions. The following companies have created their own credit ratings for businesses and each maintains its own database of companies that it has scored:

▶ **Equifax Small Business Enterprise** — Equifax, one of the three leading consumer credit bureaus, now provides business credit reports on approximately 22 million small businesses. The Small Business Credit Risk Score™ for Financial Services and for Suppliers (www. equifaxsmallbusiness.com) predicts the probability of a new or existing small business experiencing serious delinquency on financial services accounts or going bankrupt within the next 12 months. The score is based on banking and lease payment information, trade payment histories, public records, and business demographics. The numeric score for Financial Services ranges from 101 to 992. The score for Suppliers ranges from 101 to 816. You want to achieve a high score to show a low risk of delinquency. The lower the score, the higher the risk for serious delinquency. The score includes reason codes to indicate why a company achieved the rating that it did.

▶ **Experian SmartBusinessReports™** — Experian, one of the other three leading consumer credit bureaus, also provides credit data. It does *not* have a separate credit rating; its credit score is a report showing a percentage of payments made on time (current), 1-30 days late, 31-60 days late, 61-90 days late, or 91 days or more late. For example, one report might show that 25% of payments were current and 10% of payments were 1-30 days late, etc.

▶ **Credit.net** — This company, a division of InfoUSA®, provides credit reports on about 15.5 million businesses, including six million complete reports on companies with fewer than four employees (www.credit.net). It has developed its own credit score using four factors: the number of years in business, the number of employees, public records, and industry stability (the success and failure rate of businesses within an industry). The credit rating score ranges from 70 to 100; the higher numbers indicate better credit ratings. Businesses are graded on their credit history: 95 and higher is A+, 90-94 is A, 85-89 is B+, 80-84 is B, 75-79 is C+, and 70-74 is C. Scores lower than 70 indicate that there is no information on the company. The report also includes a recommended credit amount and an overall customer rating from one to five stars, with five stars being the best. The number of employees, annual sales, location, year of incorporation (if applicable), Yellow Page Ad expenditures, whether credit cards are accepted, and any corporate affiliations are also included. It is also helpful if the report lists the management directory of the company's officers and directors, along with their telephone numbers.

▶ **Accurint®Business** — The Better Business Bureau (BBB) has joined forces with LexisNexis, a leading provider of business information, to create a new business—Accurint®Business (www.accurintbusiness.com). Like Experian, this company provides business profile data and public information, as well as credit and payment data, on small, mid-sized and large companies. There is no unique credit score from this company.

▶ **ClientChecker** — ClientChecker™ (www.billingtracker.com/index.jsp) is a credit bureau that started in 2003 and is specifically geared toward assisting freelance professionals, contractor workers, and small businesses making decisions about which other businesses they'd like to work with. There is no fixed credit rating. Information is compiled by comments from member feedback.

# Summary

Business credit separate and apart from the owner's personal credit profile is vital for a business to gain access to credit on favorable terms, to do business with vendors, obtain better insurance rates, and for other reasons.

In order to build business credit, the company must become rated with a credit bureau that rates businesses. The most important such company is Dun & Bradstreet, but there are a number of other companies rating businesses today. In contrast to an individual's credit rating that is designated by a single number—the FICO score, a business's credit rating is a composite of various scores, all of which are designed to show whether it is a good credit risk.

*"Wait. Seriously? You actually DO this?"*

# Did you know?

Establishing your business's credit rating may cost a few hundred dollars up front, but is worth the investment in terms of greater access to capital when needed later on. The cost is even less than you think—it's tax deductible!

# Chapter 3

# Sources of Credit for Your Business

For many businesses the skies are never completely clear, and borrowing money can be necessary to stay in business. To strengthen your company, you want to be able to borrow money and raise funds when business opportunities arise. Poet Robert Frost said that "a bank is a place where they lend you an umbrella in fair weather and ask for it back when it begins to rain." Take the opportunities afforded to you during good times to borrow, even if you don't have a pressing need for funds. Why? Because, as Frost implies, it's easier to borrow when you don't need the money than to try for a loan when times are tough. Borrowing is an important way in which to build credit, and credit is all about your access to money.

Of course, you need good credit in most cases to qualify for borrowing. But, with little credit or even poor credit, you can obtain certain types of financing that can potentially boost your credit rating. A higher credit rating will make it easier to borrow conventionally in the future.

In order to get the right loan for your situation, it's helpful to understand your borrowing options. Not every option may be suitable for your type of business. For example, a service business cannot use factoring in most cases. Only large corporations listed on public exchanges can borrow from the public by selling their bonds.

This chapter shows you where to look for money when you need it. It explains the types of loans to consider and the types of lenders to approach. Once you've obtained the loan most suitable to your business, you'll also want to obtain the best repayment terms possible. This chapter outlines the loan terms that you'll contend with and gives you information that may help you obtain the best terms possible.

# Types of Loans

When it comes to borrowing money for your business, there are two main categories of loans: *personal loans* and *business loans*. Personal loans are based on your individual credit rating or personal resources. Lenders reviewing business loan applications will look at the business's credit, business assets, and in many cases, will also review the owner's personal credit. Which category of borrowing is better?

A business loan based solely on the business's credit is superior to all other borrowing alternatives. If things go sour over the course of the loan, the lender's only recourse is to seek damages from the business. Your personal assets and personal credit rating are fully protected. Unfortunately, for many this is a hypothetical option in the best of all possible worlds.

The next best borrowing option is a business loan secured by the owner's guarantee. While your assets are not protected in this case, you can accomplish an important business goal—building up credit for the business. In consequence, the next time the business needs money, it may be in a better position to borrow without your backing. When your business repays the loan on time, it builds up its credit rating, which future lenders will look at when considering new loans.

 *Caution:*

No matter how good your business credit, certain lenders stipulate that an owner must give her personal guarantee for a bank loan under a set amount. However, having good business credit makes it easier to obtain the loan and, usually, on more favorably repayment terms.

The following two sections describe personal and business loans in more detail, as well as the types of borrowings that fall within them.

## Personal Loans

Business owners obtain personal loans, as the name implies, from their own resources. The business is not involved in the transaction and doesn't receive funds *directly*. The owners may decide to use some or all of the proceeds for the business; they may lend the money to the company or simply make an equity contribution.

You may obtain a personal bank loan based solely on your individual credit; this type of borrowing is hardly ever used in business. Interest rates on personal loans are usually high compared with other borrowing options. There are, however, many other personal borrowing venues to consider. The beauty of borrowing personally from any of these other venues is that you can often obtain funds instantly. You do not have to fill out a loan application and then wait for approval to receive your money. For instance, if you have a home equity line of credit in place, you can tap into it whenever you need funds.

Common sources of personal loans used to finance businesses include:

▶ **Home equity loans** — Owners who have built up equity in their homes may be able to take out the equity through a home equity loan. Funds from this borrowing can usually be used for any purpose; the bank does not have to be told how you plan to use the loan proceeds. The loan can be received in one lump-sum or a line of credit with a set limit—a credit line can be tapped into whenever necessary by writing checks. If you have a business or are starting one, it's a good idea to have a home equity line of credit in place, so you can turn to it when your business cannot swing the borrowing itself.

### Note:

Unlike selling your home, which may result in taxable gain, borrowing off your home equity is not taxable—no matter what you paid for the home or how much you borrow against its current equity. Interest on personal borrowing can even be tax deductible. If funds from any source (such as home equity or a personal credit card) are used for business, the interest on the loan can be treated as fully deductible business interest. For some purchases, the interest on borrowing is treated as investment interest, such as purchasing stock in a business (Investment interest is currently deductible only to the extent of net investment income).

▶ **Credit cards** — Believe it or not, this is a highly popular way in which small business owners finance their company's needs. According to a 2003 survey by the National Small Business Association and Arthur Andersen, half of all startups are financed with credit cards, compared with just 6% financing with SBA loans. You can use your credit limit to buy things needed for your business or to obtain cash to pay the company's bills. With credit cards, you have instant access to money, but you pay dearly for this privilege. Interest rates for cash advances on business credit cards often exceed 20%. If you want to use credit cards to buy equipment and supplies and to pay business expenses, find one with the most favorable terms (see Chapter 5).

▶ **Retirement plan borrowing** — If you have a retirement plan through your company or a prior job, such as a 401(k), you can tap into your funds at your discretion. The law limits borrowing to $50,000 or 50% of your account balance, whichever is less. To obtain a loan, just ask the plan administrator. You must agree to repay the funds in equal installments over five years. Interest is usually modest and is credited to your account (you are paying yourself back). Typically you can obtain funds within a few days of your request.

▶ **Life insurance borrowing** — If you've owned permanent life insurance, such as whole life or universal life, for a number of years (usually more than 10 years), you may have built up a cash reserve that you can borrow from at favorable terms. The money is yours at your request, and you can usually receive funds within a day or two. Interest rates are low compared with commercial borrowing. You repay the loan when and to the extent you choose.

⚠ *Caution:*

**The downside to borrowing against your life insurance policy is that if you die before repaying the money, your beneficiary will receive only the net amount—what would have been received under the policy minus the outstanding loan amount and any interest owed. This type of borrowing may be helpful for stopgap purposes.**

## Business Loans

Business loans are given directly to your company from lenders. They may or may not entail any personal guarantees from the company's owners.

▶ **Commercial loan** — The most common type of business loan is a commercial bank loan. The loan may be a general purpose loan (e.g., you use the funds to launch a new product line, both purchasing inventory and marketing it) or a single purpose loan (e.g., the money is used to buy a new machine for the company). Commercial loans are discussed at greater length in Chapter 7.

▶ **Line of credit** — Like a revolving loan, there's a fixed cap on how much you can borrow with a line of credit. However, as you repay the loan, you replenish your borrowing capacity. For example, if you have a $25,000 line of credit and you borrow $5,000, your borrowing power is reduced to $20,000. But, once you repay the $5,000 (plus interest), your credit limit becomes $25,000 again. The line of credit generally runs for a fixed term, such as two years, but you can usually renew the line, or even increase the limit, if you maintain good credit.

▶ **Overdraft checking** — A variation on a line of credit, overdraft checking is tied exclusively to your business checking account. You obtain a stated credit line that you can tap into at any time by writing a check, in any amount, up to the credit limit. For example, you may have a $5,000 or $10,000 overdraft credit limit. This form of borrowing helps protect your business credit rating by ensuring adequate funds to pay your bills in a timely manner, assuming, of course, that you do not exceed your overdraft credit limit. Usually, to obtain an overdraft credit line, you must apply for it as you would any other loan. The difference is that the application process is usually a very simple one-page form without supporting documentation. The time from request to approval may take days or even weeks, depending on the lender.

▶ **Credit card borrowing** — While many small business owners start their businesses using personal credit cards, once the business becomes established, it can obtain credit cards in the company name. These credit cards typically have a line of credit that can be used to pay business expenses (see Chapter 5).

▶ **Factoring** — This is a special type of borrowing based solely on your accounts receivable (funds you are owed from sales you've already made). In effect, you're converting actualized sales into dollars using your receivables as collateral. Usually, you can obtain money within 24 to 48 hours. Factoring is discussed in more detail later in this chapter.

# Types of Lenders

Just as loans come in all sizes and shapes, so too do lenders. The good thing about lenders is their limited say in how you run your business. Unlike investors, who focus on building the business, a lender's only concern is being repaid. They don't care where you find the money to do this. They don't even care if the business is growing from year to year—unless it impacts your ability to pay off the loan.

Here are various types of lenders to explore.

## Owner as Lender

If you have the money, you can lend funds to your business and set the interest rates yourself. This can be a good loan arrangement because you can fix repayment terms that won't be onerous for the business, and at the same time, you'll make money off the interest to your loan. For instance, you can use a balloon loan, which requires the business to repay the principal to you all at once at some future date (perhaps a year or two from now when the business anticipates receipt of funds from the project's completion). This relieves the business of the burden of making principal payments throughout the term of the loan.

**Caution:**

For tax purposes, if the IRS views your "loan" as a contribution to capital, the business loses its interest deduction for payments made to you. To protect the integrity of the transaction, be sure to follow formalities by putting all loan terms (e.g., interest rate and repayment schedule) in writing and following these terms as you would with any outside lender.

## Family and Friends

Funding can be right in your own backyard. Small businesses often borrow from friends and family because of the comfort inherent in personal relationships. Your credit rating is usually not an issue, and repayment terms can be more flexible than those offered by commercial lenders. Companies, such as CircleLending at `www.circlelending.com`, can help structure an intra-family loan and will report to credit bureaus when it has been successfully paid off. However, despite these advantages, there is a significant risk involved in interfamily borrowing. If you cannot repay the money, nonpayment can damage personal relationships.

### *Note:*

When borrowing from family and friends, keep things formal. Sign a promissory note spelling out repayment terms. If you default, following formalities will enable the lender to claim a bad debt deduction for the loan. Without formalities, the loan may be viewed as a nondeductible gift, leaving the lender without the funds and no tax write-off.

## Commercial Lenders

WellsFargo, Chase, Bank of America and other commercial lenders make loans to small as well as large businesses. Years ago this wasn't so; small businesses who only wanted to borrow modest sums—under $50,000—could not look to these banks. Luckily, there is growing interest in the small-business market today, and there are more resources for loans open to them.

## SBA Loans

As a general rule, the U.S. Small Business Administration (SBA) does not make loans directly to businesses (exceptions include certain small business disaster loans). Instead, it partners with commercial lenders, community development organizations, and microlending institutions to encourage them to lend to small businesses by means of government guarantees and special loan programs.

## State and Local Governments

To encourage small businesses, particularly those that locate in economically-disadvantaged areas, many state and local governments have developed loan programs of their own. This lending is usually tied to job creation.

## Angels

You've probably heard of angels; they're the Broadway investors who back shows. The same term applies to individuals who agree to lend you money (there are also equity angels who invest in businesses rather than lend them money). Their willingness to make loans in situations where commercial lenders may not makes them an attractive lending choice. They may even make very small loans—under $5,000. Of course, there's no free lunch, and angels may charge higher interest rates than could be obtained through a commercial loan. To find an angel, go to vFinance Directory of Angel Investors (www.vfinance.com) and check whether your angel is a member of the International Angel Investors Institute at http://angelinvestors.infopoint.com. Other helpful sources include Investors' Circle (www.investorscircle.net. This is a group of private equity investors, but loans may be available here) and Angel Capital (go to www.angelcapital.org and click on **Angel Investor**.) It is important for small business owners to recognize that "venture capital" (VC), although similar to angels, is usually beyond their reach. Most VC lenders don't even look at small businesses, because their lending usually starts at $500,000 or more.

# Loan Terms

Qualifying for a loan through any of the possible lenders listed above is only step one. Next, you have to negotiate the repayment terms. Often these are dictated to you by the lender on a take-it or leave-it basis. However, sometimes you can work out terms favorable to you, particularly with family and friends.

## Time for Repayment

Usually, loans are either short-term or long-term. A short-term loan in bank parlance is one that must be repaid within a year. A long-term loan is any loan with payment terms extending beyond one year.

Commercial lenders do not customarily make long-term loans to small businesses, although exceptions are made to purchase real estate— such as a factory, office building, or strip mall. Short-term loans run only for a year or two.

## *Interest Rate*

Lenders make money on loans by charging interest for the use of their money. The interest rate you pay for borrowing money can vary widely. A couple of factors that influence interest rates are market conditions and your credit rating. The Federal Reserve sets the overnight lending rate that financial institutions pay. This rate is the point of reference for all interest rates, and any increase in this rate signals an increase in all other lending rates. In March 2007, the rate was 5.25%.

The overnight lending rate set by the Federal Reserve is *not* the rate that you'll see on the loans you may apply for. Instead, become familiar with this rate terminology that you are more likely to encounter:

▶ **Prime rate** — This is the interest rate that commercial lenders charge the largest corporate borrowers with the very best credit. The prime rate, which was 8.25% on March 22, 2007 (just 4% on May 1, 2004, and as high as 20.50% on August 1, 1981), is also used as a benchmark for fixing the rate charges to other borrowers. For example, you'll frequently see an interest rate set at "prime plus 2" (meaning the prime rate plus two percentage points).

▶ **Applicable federal rate (AFR)** — This is a rate fixed monthly by the IRS. There is a short-term, mid-term, and long-term rate adjusted on the first of each month. For example, for April 2007, the APR for short-term loans with annual compounding was 4.90%; for mid-term loans it was 4.61%; and for long-term loans, 4.81%. For an index of APRs, go to `www.irs.gov/taxpros/ lists/0,,id=98042,00.html`. Using the APR to fix the rate on a business loan is commercially acceptable and can also serve as a guideline for setting an interfamily loan rate.

 *Caution:*

Don't confuse the AFR with APR, the annual percentage rate for the loan. The APR is the actual rate you pay, after factoring in fees, discounts and other adjustments, so you can more easily compare interest rates from lender to lender.

▶ **Usurious rate** — Lenders are usually free to charge whatever they like, as long as the rate does not violate state usury laws. Some states do not have any restrictions on what lenders can charge, while others have very modest interest rate limits.

The interest rate you pay may be fixed or variable. If it is fixed, you are charged the same interest rate for the term of the loan. If it is variable, it adjusts either with market changes in interest rates or in accordance with pre-set rate adjustments under the terms of the loan. For example, the rate may adjust in tandem with market changes and adjustments to the prime rate. If the prime rate increases, your loan rate adjusts accordingly. If the prime rate decreases, your loan rate declines. A preset rate adjustment works differently. Your loan terms may call for a set interest rate the first six months of the loan, but the rate will escalate after that time, regardless of market changes.

## Secured or Unsecured Loans

An unsecured loan is granted solely on your promise to repay. You can obtain this type of loan only if your credit rating elicits the lender's confidence. In contrast, a secured loan is backed by collateral, usually of value equal to the amount of the loan. Collateral is explained below.

## Collateral

Collateral is property designated as security for the lender. If you don't repay the money you owe, the lender can seize this property to satisfy the loan. Having collateral may enable you to obtain a loan you might otherwise lose because of a mediocre credit report.

A lender may take physical possession of some types of collateral, such as certificates for securities, until the loan is repaid. Usually, you retain possession of property designated as collateral, such as machinery, although you are restricted in what you can do with it. You can't simply sell it, because it diminishes the lender's recourse in case of a default. Be sure that you're certain whether you can dispose of collateral, whether you need the lender's approval for a sale, and whether you must segregate collateral from your other property.

What can you use as collateral for a loan? Just because something is valuable to you doesn't mean that a lender considers it equally as valuable. Table 3.1 from SBA's Web site shows how much of an asset type can be used as collateral for a loan.

| Collateral type | Bank | SBA |
|---|---|---|
| House | 75% of market value minus any mortgage balance | 80% of market value minus any mortgage balance |
| Car | Nothing | Nothing |
| Truck and heavy equipment | 50% of depreciated value | 50% of depreciated value |
| Office equipment | Nothing | Nothing |
| Furniture and fixtures | 50% of depreciated value | 50% of depreciated value |
| Inventory (perishables) | Nothing | Nothing |
| Receivables | 75% of receivables under 90 days | 50% of receivables under 90 days |
| Stocks and bonds | 50%-90% | 50%-90% |
| Mutual funds | Nothing | Nothing |
| CDs | 100% | 100% |
| IRAs | Nothing | Nothing |
| Jewelry | Nothing | Nothing |
| Other | 10%-50% | 10%-50% |

**Table 3.1:** SBA's Approximated Values of Collateral Types (Source: SBA).

## How Repayment is Made

Loans can be repaid in installments, typically with monthly payments, or in a lump sum. A lump sum is called a *balloon payment*.

### Note:

If you borrow from the bank with which you have your business checking account and the loan calls for monthly payments, you can arrange to have payments debited automatically to your bank. This not only is a convenience to you, but may also warrant a slightly lower interest rate.

# Trade Accounts

If you sell on terms of 30 days, 60 days, or more, you put yourself in the position of becoming a collection agency as well as a bank. Once you've completed the work needed to finish the sale, you must wait to collect your money on the terms you set. While you wait for your money, you effectively become a banker because you've helped your customers obtain what they need from you on an interest-free basis.

## How Factoring Works

Using a financing method called *factoring*, you can turn your trade accounts into money immediately, rather than waiting out the collection period. Find a factor—preferably one specializing in your industry, such as apparel or trucking. Then, send your invoices to the factor and arrange terms (what portion of the invoice you will receive upon collection and what portion the factor keeps). Usually, you can obtain your money within 24 to 48 hours. The amount of money you'll receive from a factoring company depends on certain variables, including: your volume of business, the average size of each invoice, the creditworthiness of your customers, your terms of sale (e.g., net 30 days), and industry conditions. Typically, you can receive 80% to 90% of the amount of the invoices submitted.

When the factor collects on a receivable, it keeps a portion and pays you the balance. The factoring fee (also called an origination fee) can run 2% to 4% of the loan balance. In addition, you'll pay either an interest charge on the funds advanced to you or a factoring fee for each 30-day period, which may be more than an interest charge.

## Note:

Your business credit rating has no impact on what you can borrow through factoring. Only your customers' ratings matter; their ratings can work for or against you.

## Other Trade Account Financing

Factoring is not the only way in which to use trade accounts to raise immediate cash for your business. For example, Advance Me, Inc. (www.advanceme.com) can lend money to just about any business that regularly accepts credit cards. The loan application is simple, and there's no application fee. To qualify, you usually need to have been in business for at least 12 months and have at least $1,700 of credit card sales per month. If approved, you receive funds within 10 to 14 business days. You do not make any payments to the company; it is repaid solely through your credit card collections. But because of its cut in your collections, you effectively pay 30% or more interest to obtain money through their company.

# Private or Public Offerings

Large corporations can raise money by enabling the public to become lenders to them. This is done by selling bonds to investors. The public who buys the bonds becomes lenders to the corporation that sold them. The corporation, as borrower, repays the principal of the bonds plus interest.

Privately-held companies do not have the same access to the public as corporations listed on exchanges.

# Using Loans to Build Credit

Borrowing is good for your business credit as long as you are a good borrower. If you repay what you borrow on time and in full, you will build up a positive history of repayment. As you look to borrow in the future, lenders will more likely give you favorable terms of repayment on your new loan.

This concept of borrowing and repaying loans to build credit applies to just about any type of loan. So, repaying your bank loan and paying off your borrowing on a business credit card are both important ways in which to build up credit.

Factoring holds a special place in building credit. The arrangement itself has no direct impact on your business credit. However, if you use factoring to turn your trade accounts into cash, you can use that money to pay off your obligations. This will build upon your business credit. Moreover, factoring is a form of borrowing that does not show up on your business balance sheet as a loan. So if you are applying for commercial financing, any outstanding factoring will not be a detriment to loan qualification.

# Summary

There are many options for borrowing money for your business. These include tapping various personal resources as well as looking to business lenders. In selecting the source of financing and arranging repayment, be sure to understand repayment terms. Also, understand how your credit rating may impact these terms. Being a "good" borrower is a key way in which to build up business credit that you can use to obtain better loan terms in the future.

*"As you can see, our repayment terms are quite reasonable."*

# Establishing Credit for Your Business

# Chapter 4

# Business Credit Building Basics

Now you should fully understand the importance of building business credit. If you want your business to stand on its own, the company must build and maintain a separate credit identity from its owners. You can do this passively, which can take considerable time, or actively, which can enable you to use business credit much faster.

Like personal credit, your company's credit depends on many factors, including years in business, company assets, and payment history. You can build business credit by nurturing these factors. As a small or mid-sized business, you can also hurry things along by proactively building credit.

In this chapter, you will learn about the building blocks of credit and strategies for optimizing them to your advantage. This chapter also explains how business credit is built if you do nothing (passive credit building) and what you can do to build credit quickly (active credit building), including the first step: obtaining a D-U-N-S® number from Dun & Bradstreet.

## *Passive Credit Building*

As your company operates from year to year, you are building business credit whether you realize it or not. Certain creditors—usually large companies, including banks, credit card companies, utilities, and even government agencies—routinely report your payment activities to D&B and other credit bureaus. Like FBI files, you have a credit file stored away. But unlike FBI files that are secret, others may access your credit file if they ask for it. They may have to pay a credit bureau for the information, but you can't block someone from accessing it.

You can ensure that you create a favorable credit picture by having a sound payment history, a solid balance sheet, and a safe workplace to avoid legal actions against you. Follow the steps discussed below on the building blocks of credit.

# Active Credit Building

Instead of waiting for D&B or another credit bureau to find out about your company and compile a credit history on the business, you can take on a proactive role to build your credit history. This is explained in Chapter 8.

# Building Blocks of Credit

No single factor is used to determine a company's creditworthiness. By the same token, in most cases, no single factor will undermine its creditworthiness. Your business's credit profile depends on an amalgam of several factors, including:

▶ Paying your bills on time

▶ Having a strong balance sheet

▶ Staying out of legal trouble

▶ Creating and maintaining a strong business identity

Lenders may place emphasis on one or more of these factors when looking into your credit history. For example, if you are looking for a commercial loan, the lending officer may put considerable emphasis on your balance sheet. A vendor deciding whether to do business with you is less concerned about your balance sheet; he wants to know primarily whether you pay your bills on time. Insurance companies that take credit into account when rating policies may factor in your litigation history.

## Paying on Time

Paying your bills when they fall due is probably the single most important factor in determining your business credit. When you owe money to a vendor and fail to pay on time, that vendor may stop doing business with you. Or, if the vendor continues to deal with you, the terms of future transactions may fall out of your favor. Instead of 30 day net, you may be required to pay in advance, in whole, or in part immediately following the transaction.

When you owe money to large corporations, such as banks, credit card companies and utilities, you should be vigilant about paying your bills on time. Your failure to pay by the due date will probably be reported to a credit bureau, such as Dun & Bradstreet. This will directly impact your credit rating by the bureau. Obviously, this can have a wider effect on your business than failing to pay a bill to a smaller vendor on time.

What is timely payment? Timely payment means complying with the terms of the sale. Sometimes payment is due immediately upon receipt of the invoice. In other cases, payment may be due on fixed terms—within 30, 60, or 90 days following receipt of the invoice. Paying some bills early, say within 30 days of a 60-day term, will not offset a separate late payment. That late payment still becomes part of your credit history.

An occasional late payment will not destroy an otherwise good credit rating. Most companies that report to credit bureaus only do so when payment is more than 30 days beyond the due date. But a pattern of poor payment habits—repeatedly being more than 30 days late—can become a black mark on your creditworthiness.

## Strategies for Paying on Time

Every business experiences cash flow problems from time to time. Your customers may be tardy in paying you, leaving you short of cash to pay your own bills. Develop practices to ensure that you can meet your obligations regardless of cash flow problems. Here are some ways to do this:

▶ **Overdraft checking** — Obtain this borrowing option on your business checking account so you'll have funds available to pay your bills on time, even if you temporarily experience a cash flow crunch. You'll pay interest on this borrowing, but it is a small price to pay to protect your creditworthiness.

▶ **Automated payments** — If some of your payments are due on a regular basis (such as rent, estimated taxes, and insurance premiums) consider setting up online payments to automate your bill-paying. Small business owners can schedule their federal estimated tax payments up to one year in advance through the Electronic Federal Tax Payment System (EFTPS) (www. eftps.gov). Overdraft checking can ensure that your account has sufficient funds on hand to satisfy the payments you make.

▶ **Negotiate new terms before payment is due** — If you realize that you won't be able to meet a pending obligation, don't ignore it. Instead, talk with your creditor to ask for more time to pay. In many cases, you may be granted more time—often a month—to pay up. This way you'll avoid having reports sent to D&B or other credit bureaus about a late payment. You may wish to simply change the payment date to a different time that coincides with your receivables. For instance, if you regularly receive payments on your receivables around the 7th of each month, you may wish to arrange a payment date of the 21st. This will give you enough time to deposit payments you received in your bank account and send your check in the mail. Alternatively, if you're experiencing a cash flow problem, arrange for partial payment on time with additional time to complete the payment.

▶ **Prioritize payments** — If you can't negotiate with all creditors to wait for payment, then pay those accounts that will report late payments to D&B or other credit bureaus. This will help protect your credit history. Of course, you must temper this strategy with the need to maintain good relationships with particular creditors. Be sure to pay vendors whose business is vital to yours, even if you don't think the vendor will report a late payment. You don't want to spoil your relationship with them.

▶ **Authorize payment by phone** — Some companies (such as insurance companies, utilities, and credit card companies) can accept payment by telephone. You can authorize a payment by providing the company with your bank account number and the bank's routing number, and the funds are immediately debited from your account. The company, not the bank, can charge you an extra fee to use this payment method. But if the due date arrives and you have not paid, you can avoid a late payment report on your credit history by making a last-minute transfer.

## *Building a Balance Sheet*

A balance sheet is a snap shot of your business's assets and liabilities at any given time. Assets include equipment and property you own, as well as accounts receivable and other money owed to you. Liabilities include mortgages, loans, and accounts payable—money your company owes.

When you apply for a commercial loan, the lender usually looks at your company's financial statements, which includes a balance sheet. A solid balance sheet—with assets exceeding liabilities—is important to be viewed as a good credit risk by a commercial lender.

## Strategies for Building a Better Balance Sheet

Business decisions you make throughout the year can affect your balance sheet. If you anticipate the need to borrow money from a commercial lender, expect to have your balance sheet scrutinized. Here are some strategies to keep in mind to improve the look of your balance sheet:

▶ **Retain cash** — When you know that your balance sheet will be examined, keep cash on hand rather than spending it on anything other than hard assets.

▶ **Wait to write-off bad receivables** — One of your business's assets is accounts receivable. Sometimes these assets go uncollected. Again, if you want to make your balance sheet look good, you can delay abandoning collection efforts so the receivables remain an asset on your balance sheet.

▶ **Manage inventory** — If you are a manufacturer, keep in mind that finished goods are worth more on your balance sheet than raw materials. Convert your raw materials before letting potential lenders view your balance sheet.

▶ **Lease rather than purchase equipment** — If you lease equipment, the lease or rental fees are treated as off-balance sheet financing rather than as a balance sheet liability. Therefore, the lease and rental fees are not included in a balance sheet. However, a lease-to-buy contract is an exception to this rule; it is a capital lease. If you do decide to purchase equipment, you gain an asset for your balance sheet, but if you finance the purchase, the debt is carried as an offsetting liability on the balance sheet.

## Note:

Work with a knowledgeable accountant who can advise you on other ways to not only improve your company's profitability, but also to upgrade your balance sheet. Make sure your accountant adheres to generally accepted accounting principals (GAAP) when preparing your books and records—something commercial lenders may look for.

## Avoiding Lawsuits

Many small-business owners fear being sued more than just about any other business challenge. There are sound reasons for this concern. According to the National Federation of Independent Business (NFIB), small companies are easy targets for frivolous lawsuits because they are more willing than larger companies to settle claims. It can cost $100,000 in legal fees to fight them, which many small businesses cannot afford. The U.S. Chamber of Commerce reported that lawsuits and liability insurance cost businesses $128.8 billion every year. An estimated 4.4 million small businesses (those with annual sales between $1 million and $4.9 million) pay more than half those costs—44% of which is paid out-of-pocket rather than through insurance! While there are measures in Congress that would provide reform to actions against small businesses (e.g., limited damages against a small business for noneconomic loss), nothing has yet been enacted.

Lawsuits are a matter of a public record and become part of your credit record as well. There is nothing you can do to keep a judgment from a lawsuit off your credit history. Your best defense is a good offense. Avoid lawsuits in the first place so there won't be any judgments on your credit report.

### Strategies for Avoiding Lawsuits

Unfortunately, there's nothing that can be done to bullet-proof your company against legal actions. You can, however, take measures to reduce the likelihood that you'll become a target. Here are some ideas to help you:

> ▶ **Keep safety in mind** — Making your environment a safer place to work will reduce claims against you by employees, customers, and other business visitors. When necessary, work with the Occupational Safety and Health Administration (OSHA) (www.osha.gov) to get tips on how to keep your workplace safe.

> ▶ **Avoid employment actions** — A growing area of litigation concerns grievances by employees for discrimination, sexual harassment, wrongful termination and other workplace injuries. Learn what's appropriate and what isn't. A good resource to help you is the U.S. Department of Labor (www.dol.gov/dol/audience/aud-employers.htm).

▶ **Work with attorneys** — Consulting fees to get an answer to a particular question may seem high, but they're low when compared with the costs of litigation. For example, work with an attorney to protect your intellectual property, a growing area of litigation. You don't want to pour thousands of dollars into marketing a product whose name may already be the property of another company. You'll lose not only your marketing dollars, but also your profits and legal fees when you are sued for wrongfully using the other company's name.

▶ **Work with insurance agents** — Insurance experts can help you assess your risks, so that you not only carry adequate insurance but also take steps to reduce your liability exposure.

If you have had a judgment or lien (e.g., tax lien or mechanics lien) filed against your company, try to settle matters as quickly as possible. These items stay on your company's credit history for some time (perhaps as long as seven years), so the faster you resolve them, the sooner they'll disappear from your credit report.

## Years in Business

It's just a fact that the longer you're in business, the more creditworthy you become. It stands to reason that if you've been able to make it, you probably have done so by satisfying your creditors. If you had not been able to meet your obligations, you would have folded, or your creditors would have forced you to shut down long ago.

There's nothing you can do to hurry time and add years to your company's life. Just recognize that if you are a start up, the other building blocks of credit will weigh more heavily than if you've been around for three, five, or more years.

## Other Factors

To build business credit, you must show that you are indeed in business (and are not just trying to create a business façade). Various non-financial factors are used to rate your company's credit. These include:

▶ **Employer identification number** — The business must have a separate tax ID number, called a federal employer identification number (EIN). Usually, a company obtains this number for tax reasons.

**Note:**

A sole proprietor may not be required to have an EIN for tax filing and can use the owner's Social Security number on a tax return, but it is highly advisable to obtain an EIN. The EIN is a key building block of a company's credit profile. It is easy to request an EIN at no cost from the IRS. You can apply online (www.irs.gov/businesses/small/ article/0,,id=102767,00.html) and obtain one immediately.

▶ **Business premises** — It is helpful for a business to have its own location, but even a home-based business can establish credit. Home-based businesses can facilitate the credit-building process by having a separate business phone number and fax number. Doing so gives the business a presence in the yellow pages, a source that may be checked by credit rating companies.

▶ **Business licenses and permits** — The business should obtain all required state and local licenses and permits. For example, if the business is a sole proprietorship, it should file a "DBA" ("doing business as") form to establish the company name. Say George Wang has a consulting business operating under the name of Helpful Hand Technologies. Legally, the company and the owner are one and the same. But the business's vendors and customers are used to dealing with it through its DBA, Helpful Hand Technologies. Reporting payments to the credit bureau can become confusing without a DBA.

▶ **Business organization** — Businesses that take formal steps to organize under state law as corporations or limited liability companies may be viewed as better credit risks than less formal entities, such as sole proprietorships and partnerships. However, sole proprietorships and partnerships are not precluded from building business credit; it just may be a little harder to do so.

# *Summary*

Many factors are taken into account in determining a company's credit rating. These include not only its bill-paying history, but also how it is set up, how long you've been in business and several other important factors.

Be sure to understand these factors and take appropriate measures to improve your standing. For example, take steps to avoid lawsuits where possible and to upgrade the appearance of your balance sheet.

You can build your company's credit profile on a passive or active basis. Becoming proactive accelerates the establishment of a separate business credit for your company.

# Did you know?

You can maintain better control over your business bank account by using online banking services. This enables you to review your account daily to ensure that transactions, such as your daily credit card receipts, have been properly recorded.

# Chapter 5

# Using Credit Card Borrowing to Build Credit

Credit cards aren't just for charging business meals and travel. They can also be used to finance the purchase of equipment or obtain cash in a crunch. Long before a company can qualify for a commercial bank loan, it may be able to borrow money through a credit card.

Obtaining a business credit card is not only a way to obtain the goods and services a company needs, it's also an important way to build a company's credit. This is because the credit card company usually reports payment activities to credit bureaus, such as Dun & Bradstreet, helping a business build a credit history.

Like bank loans, business credit cards can be obtained on the basis of the business's credit alone, or a combination of the owner's and business's credit. Ideally, you want the company to apply for a card on its own credit.

This chapter covers business credit card basics, including the uses of a credit card and how to obtain one. It lists business card options and factors to use in choosing a card or cards. It also shows how to use credit cards as substitute to bank loans—how much you can qualify for and what this will cost you.

# What's a Business Credit Card?

Many entrepreneurs help to finance and run a business using their personal credit cards. This may be a necessary step in getting started. But once your business is up and running, think about getting a business credit card.

According to a Tower Report, over two thirds of small businesses regularly use credit cards, but only 40% have business credit cards (the others are using owners' personal credit cards for business purchases). Statistics from the U.S. Census Bureau for 2003 (the most recent year for which statistics are available) show that 38.5% of businesses with 20 employees have business credit cards. Continued use of an owner's and/or employee's personal credit card to make business purchases is generally not a good idea for several reasons:

▶ **Business credit** — This practice does not help the company build and maintain a separate business credit history. Only the maintenance of a good payment history on a business credit card will enhance the company's credit rating.

▶ **Higher credit limit** — If you rely on personal credit cards to make business purchases, you may not be able to charge the things your company needs. Business cards typically have higher credit limits than those offered on personal cards. A business card with a credit limit of $50,000, gives a business owner greater liberty to make purchases for his company than his personal credit card, which may only have a $15,000 limit.

▶ **Accounting and tax problems** — Using a personal card for business expenses can create bookkeeping and tax problems for the business and its owners. A corporate owner who charges legitimate company expenses on her personal credit card may prevent the corporation from deducting the expenses. If she wants to deduct them on her personal tax return, they are treated as a miscellaneous itemized business expense, which is deductible only if such miscellaneous deductions exceed 2% of her adjusted gross income. Even if these miscellaneous items are deductible for regular tax purposes, this may trigger or increase an owner's personal alternative minimum tax.

Like your personal credit card, a business credit card is a charge card issued in the company's name. The face of the card may show both the company name and the name of the person authorized on the card. For example, the card may read:

> Brown and Martinez, LLC
> Edward Martinez

You can receive multiple cards under the company's business credit card (there may or may not be an additional charge), so each owner and authorized employee can have his or her own card. Or you may wish to use separate business credit cards for specified purposes; a business may have two credit cards, one for employees' travel and entertainment (T&E) expenses and the other to be used at the owners' discretion.

Issuers sometimes call business credit cards "corporate cards." Don't let the name fool you. You can use a corporate card regardless of how your business is organized. For example, you can obtain a corporate card for your sole proprietorship, partnership, or limited liability company.

Today, it is virtually impossible to run a business without a business credit card. It is a convenient method of payment, and one that is expected in many situations. For example, if your company makes online purchases, in most cases it must use a credit card to complete the transaction.

## Uses of Business Credit Cards

Obviously, the company can use the business credit card to charge goods and services. Taking a customer out to lunch, buying needed supplies, or paying for gasoline for a company car are just a few popular uses for a business credit card. But these are not the only ways in which a card can be useful to your business. Other uses for having business credit cards include:

> ▶ **Financing** — Instead of using a bank or other structured financing to purchase equipment the company needs, such as a computer or office furniture, you can use a credit card to obtain them immediately. Instead of paying off the credit card balance in full, the company can make partial payments as it is able. The advantage to using a credit card is the convenience of the financing. Nothing has to be arranged in advance, and you decide how quickly to pay off the loan (as long as you pay at least the minimum amount required each month). The downside is the cost of

borrowing; interest rates and other charges can make this financing more costly than conventional borrowing.

▶ **Cash advances** — If you are experiencing a cash flow problem, you can use a business credit card to raise extra cash. Check your cash advance limit on the card, which may be less than the limit for charging purchases. Once again, this type of borrowing is convenient, but can be costly.

▶ **Segregate business from personal expenses** — Simplify company bookkeeping and keep your personal expenses out of the mix. Annual statements from the credit card company can even assist in tax preparation. These statements group your annual charges in categories (e.g., business meals) to simplify your tax preparation.

▶ **Employee expense accounts** — Using a company credit card can produce a tax advantage. Give employees company credit cards that can be used to charge pre-authorized expenses (e.g., business travel costs) and have the company adopt an "accountable plan." An accountable plan is an IRS-sanctioned reimbursement arrangement in which employees are not taxed on reimbursements and the company owes no employment tax on these amounts. One of the key requirements of the plan is that employees must substantiate their expenses to the company, and the company credit card can be used to satisfy this requirement (for more on accountable plans, see IRS Publication 463, Travel, Entertainment, Gift, and Car Expenses, at www.irs. gov).

▶ **Employee medical benefits** — If your company offers its employees health reimbursement accounts (HRAs) or flexible spending accounts (FSAs) to cover medical costs of employees, spouses, and dependents on a tax-advantaged basis, company credit or debit cards can be given to employees. The use of the cards is restricted to covered medical costs (for more on these medical plans, see IRS Publication 969, Health Savings Accounts and Other Tax-Favored Health Plans, at www.irs.gov).

▶ **Added benefits** — Credit cards offer an array of add-ons that your business may value. Various credit cards offer trip assistance services, which are worth considering if you travel extensively on business. If you do business in Europe and regularly travel there, acquire one of the MasterCard credit cards that offers a VAT (Value Added Tax) Reclaim Service on its cards, which is an efficient way for your business to reclaim any VAT it might have paid. To protect yourself from unauthorized charges on your business card, QuickBooks Platinum Plus for Business MasterCard offers protection up to $100,000 for employee misuse of the card.

# Applying for a Business Credit Card

Just open your mailbox and you're sure to find one or more offers for business credit cards. Some may even say they are "pre-approved." Receiving a credit card offer, especially one that says pre-approved, is a good indication that you can command a business credit card. However, the credit limit you receive is not yet fixed. To establish a credit limit, you must submit the credit card application. The credit card company will examine many factors to not only approve a card issuance, but also to set a spending limit and, where applicable, a limit on a line of credit. The credit card company may also set an interest rate dependent on your business's credit history.

Applications can be completed online through secure Web sites or mailed. You may wish to apply for a business credit card through the bank with which you maintain your business bank account. The card can be issued more quickly and sometimes even automatically because the bank already knows you as a customer. Applying for a business card enhances your banking relationship, something that can prove useful when applying for a commercial loan through this bank.

Credit card issuers consider a number of factors when granting authorization and setting purchase and cash advance limits. These include:

▶ **Credit history** — The issuer will check your company's credit rating through D&B or another rating service. If your company has a poor or nonexistent credit history, it may be denied a card based solely on the company's credit. Some issuers may give you a company card despite a poor credit history if an owner gives his personal guarantee.

▶ **Annual sales** — Some cards are only issued to businesses with sales exceeding a set amount (e.g., $100,000 or $2 million annually). Find out about any such thresholds before even applying for these cards.

You are not limited to one business credit card. You may wish to obtain more than one card for certain purposes. For instance, you may want a second credit card used solely by employees for their expense account charges. Two or three business credit cards may be useful. Keep in mind, however, the impact that multiple cards (with multiple borrowing power) may have on your credit rating. Just like having multiple personal credit cards, applying for too many business cards can adversely impact your credit history.

# Lines of Credit on Business Credit Cards

There is no such thing as a standard line of credit on a business credit card. Card issuers may set publicized limits on a line of credit, but this does not mean you automatically qualify for the full line when you obtain card authorization.

### Lending Criteria

What do credit card companies base your credit limit on? Each company sets its own criteria for fixing your line of credit on the business credit card. Of course, your credit lines depends on your credit profile.

The process for fixing a line of credit on a credit card is practically the same as the one used for any commercial financing. The credit card company will review the company's credit rating (if the company has one) and often will require that an owner submit his personal credit information and guarantee for small businesses. The only difference between applying for a credit card line of credit versus a bank loan is the fact that no financial statements or business plans are required.

Some credit card companies may authorize a set limit, as much as $25,000, based on usual inquiries about your credit rating, but require additional information (e.g., financial statements) if you want higher limits. Additional authorization may take additional time.

# How Big a Line of Credit Can You Get?

When asked how big a line you should request, your instinctual response might be "as much as possible." But your initial reaction would be wrong. You must be able to manage the line you obtain in order to maintain a good credit rating.

Your financial needs, company assets, and general shape of your business finances determine the amount of the credit line that you should request (and the credit line that you will qualify for). You must think ahead; the money you request today must be sufficient to meet your upcoming needs but manageable in terms of payment.

It is highly advisable that the line on the credit card be small enough so that you can pay it off for at least one month during the year, a practice that demonstrates a solid business. If you can't pay off the line you obtain and use for at least one month during a 12-month period, future lenders may think that you borrowed too much, or that your sales are not what you had expected, or that you are otherwise having financial difficulties.

# Small Business Credit Card Selections

Most major credit card issuers offer business credit cards, many of which are geared to small businesses. In selecting a credit card, compare the following features:

▶ **Annual fee** — Many credit cards have no annual fee, while others have a fee up to $100. The credit card companies may tout the fact that their product has no annual fee, but this factor alone should not be the deciding factor in making your credit card selection.

▶ **Interest rate** — If you are using the card merely as a payment convenience and expect to pay off the balance each month, the card's interest rate should not be a deciding factor in credit card selection. However, the interest rate is an important factor if you anticipate using the card for cash advances, balance transfers, and equipment financing. The card can have several interest rates: a regular interest rate on unpaid monthly balances, a separate rate on cash advances, and a rate for balances transferred from other credit cards (usually an attractive zero or low percentage rate for a limited period, such as six months).

▶ **Credit line** — If you want to use the card as a source for operating capital, you'll need a card that provides you with a credit line. As mentioned earlier in this chapter, there is no "standard" credit line; different cards offer different limits on credit lines, but the one you obtain depends on your company's credit history.

▶ **Grace period** — This is a polite term for the card's billing cycle. If you pay your bill in full within this period, you avoid any interest charges. If you fail to pay in full, interest starts to accrue. A typical grace period on a credit card is 25 days.

▶ **Rewards** — Some cards offer special rebates and rewards for certain purchases. For example, you may receive cash back (e.g., 1% or 3% for every dollar you charge), free gasoline (e.g., 3% or 5% for every gasoline purchase you make), frequent flyer miles, or other benefits each time you use your card for a designated purchase. There may or may not be a fee for participating in a rewards program in addition to any annual fee for the card itself.

 *Caution:*

There are usually added fees and charges for various card-related services, such as using convenience checks from the credit card companies. Many cards have a charge for each additional card issued. If, for example, you want five people to use the company card, you'll pay the fee times four (there is no charge for the first card). Fees and charges also accrue on late payments and defaults.

Most importantly, always read the fine print at the time you apply for the card, as well as any new fine print on mailings that you receive from the credit card company from time to time. An advertisement or solicitation for a credit card may claim to have no annual fee, but the fine print may explain that this freebie is limited to customers who meet certain criteria.

You can compare more than a dozen business credit card choices at CreditCard.com (www.creditcards.com/business.php), CardRatings.com (www.cardratings.com, click on **Business Cards** under **Card Reports**), LowCards.com (www.lowcards.com/busi nesscards.asp) and MoneySearch.com (www.moneysearch.com/creditcards/busines screditcards.html).

**FREE** *Bonus:*

Obtain a listing of the most popular small business credit cards and their features when you register your book at www.rationalpress.com.

## When to Use Secured Business Credit Cards

If your company does not have any business credit or has a poor credit history, you may have difficulty obtaining a company card. But there is a solution, a secured business credit card can establish or re-build business credit.

The amount of credit you command through the card is linked to bank account created as collateral for the card. Usually, the cardholder must deposit 100% of the credit line in this account, depending on the card issuer. For example, if you have $20,000 in your collateral bank account, you gain a $20,000 line of credit.

For example, Wells Fargo's Business Secured Card (a MasterCard), can provide a credit line up to $50,000. You must maintain a collateral deposit account at Wells Fargo equal to the amount of your credit line. You earn interest on the account, but the interest earned is considerably lower than the interest you pay on borrowed funds. On this card, you earn 2.5% interest on your collateral deposit account for the first year, but you pay prime plus 9.9% APR on purchases and prime plus 12% (with a minimum of 19.8%) APR on cash advances.

Is a secured business credit card a good idea? It can be helpful in establishing a solid credit history for your company, but it is only viable if you have the financial ability to tie up funds in a collateral account. Even if you can afford to open a secured business credit card, it should only be used as a short-term solution (probably no more than a year) because of the high cost of borrowing.

*Caution:*

**If you are using a secured card because you cannot obtain an unsecured one, beware of false and deceptive advertisers. There may be hidden fees and charges by companies offering to help you arrange for a secured card. Stick with a known company, such as Wells Fargo and Orchard Bank, and obtain the card directly from the issuer (do not use a middleman).**

## When to Use "Bonus" Cards

In addition to their convenience, business credit cards can be used to obtain free things, from gasoline to frequent flyer miles. When selecting a business credit card, determine whether one offering cash backs or other freebies is a good choice for your situation.

Your card selection should depend on what you're using the card for. In most cases, rewards cards have higher interest rates because, as the old saying goes, you don't get something for nothing. If you plan to use the card for cash or you don't expect to pay off the balance each month, the give-backs cost you money in higher interest payments and probably aren't worth what you receive. As a rule of thumb:

► **Use a give-back card** if you pay the balance in full each month.

► **Don't use a give-back card** if you use the card for financing purchases or obtaining cash.

So-called rebate or reward cards may be desirable if you do a lot of traveling for business. You can build frequent flyer miles to obtain free travel or travel upgrades, which can amount to considerable savings for your business.

# Summary

Business credit cards serve a number of very useful purposes for your company. They not only help to build up a credit profile, but they can also be a ready source of cash or financing.

When applying for business cards, understand the terms and conditions that apply. Decide which features are important to your business when making a card selection.

If you have poor credit and cannot open a business credit card immediately, you should consider opening a secured business credit card temporarily. It's an effective way to build credit despite the drawbacks that it entails.

*"Don't worry about it, this will be
good for the company credit."*

# Did you know?

When shopping for a business credit card, start with your business's bank. An existing banking relationship can ensure credit card approval and may entitle you to a greater line of credit on the card than you could get from a bank that you have no relationship with.

# Chapter 6

# Relying on Vendor Advances

When we think of credit, the first thing that often comes to mind is a bank loan or a credit card. But one of the most common forms of credit used by small businesses is making purchases from vendors without making an immediate payment in full.

This chapter covers the financial aspects of transactions you make with other businesses to acquire the goods, materials, and services you need to run and grow your company. You'll learn how to obtain credit from your vendors and suppliers, what it will cost you, and how to use it to build your company's credit profile. Some vendor transactions involve lengthy payment terms and interest payments; other transactions require prompt payment within 10 to 30 days. This chapter explains the payment terms associated with long-term vendor financing, leasing, and purchasing so that you can decide which option best suites your business's needs.

## *Vendor (Trade) Credit*

Business-to-business dealings (B2B), which are transactions between companies and manufacturers, wholesalers or suppliers, are often done on credit. (B2C is business to consumer; B2G is business to government). To grease the wheels of this type of commerce, a business will often let you obtain its goods or services right away, even though you pay for them in whole or in part later on. The arrangement, referred to as trade or vendor credit, is a win-win for both parties. You obtain immediately and conveniently the things you need, and the vendor increases its sales.

For example, it is common practice for a contractor to maintain a store account with a hardware store or building supply company. Whenever necessary, the contractor can obtain the lumber and materials he needs for his ongoing projects without worrying about paying the vendor immediately. The cost is put on the contractor's account, and he'll receive a monthly bill to settle the account at that time. The bill will usually require payment upon receipt or perhaps net 10 days.

> ## *Note:*
>
> **Net 10 days means payment is required within 10 days of the invoice date. Another common invoice term is EOM (end of the month). Payments on an account billed EOM are due the month following the accrued charges. For example, the contractor's charges at the building supply company in May must be paid by the end of June.**

Vendor credit can get more complicated than the arrangement described between the contractor and the building supply company—the terms of payment in a B2B transaction can be anything agreed upon in advance by the two parties. One retailer may purchase inventory from a wholesaler under net 30 terms while a second retailer may purchase from the same wholesaler for net 60 terms. Usually, there is no interest charged if payment is made within the required time.

Whether another business will provide credit to your business and how it determines your payment terms varies widely from vendor to vendor. Many vendors require you to complete their own credit applications and may perform both personal and business credit checks. Numerous vendors will also require an owner to give a personal guarantee for any credit extended to the company. Not all vendors, however, will place such emphasis on credit profiles. Other vendors are more informal and will simply extend credit to a company that it knows (especially if the company is well established and has been in business for a number of years).

Despite the various ways that vendor credit is arranged, the concept is always same; it is done to encourage other businesses to make purchases, and it is a common business practice.

Before stepping into a trade agreement, research the terms with great care. There may be a hidden cost to using trade credit. Unless you are charged interest for the time you are effectively using the vendor's money (a cost you can readily see and easily quantify), you may be charged a higher price for the goods and supplies you purchase as a way to offset the cost of making the advances to you (something that can be difficult to calculate). If the vendor's prices seem unduly high, shop around and arrange trade credit with another vendor or supplier.

# Arranging Payment Terms

There's no such thing as standard terms. Everything is up for grabs. The stronger your company is financially and the better your relationship is with the vendor, the better the terms will be. If you've been dealing with a particular supplier for years and have never failed to pay on time, you can probably command the best terms this supplier offers. For example, you may be given 30 days (expressed as "net 30") to pay because the supplier is confident that you will keep your promise and pay on time.

You can arrange for trade credit at any point in a relationship. You may initially be required to pay cash to purchase what you need, but once you've developed a relationship with a supplier, that business may be willing to advance you credit.

Terms may be negotiated with your vendor/supplier or simply presented to you on a take-it-or-leave-it basis. If you find a particular term objectionable, try to negotiate for something better. If you think that any of your payments terms are questionable, be sure to have them reviewed by an attorney.

## Common Trade Credit Terms

Terms are usually stated in an invoice or in a more complex agreement, depending on the situation. The following are some of the common terms found when arranging trade credit:

▶ **Net terms** — Net 10 days, net 30 days, or net any other period effectively operates as a loan for the net period. While you have possession of the property immediately, the vendor expects you to pay up within the net period.

▶ **Interest rates** — Interest rates are used in two instances: when you make payments over time (e.g., installments) and when you are late in making scheduled payments. For example, if you pay a net 30 invoice 30 days late, you usually owe interest for the 30 day period that you were late. The interest rate is arbitrarily fixed by the vendor, as long as it does not violate state usury laws (some states put limits on interest charges).

▶ **Installment payments** — Many elements must be taken into consideration when fixing installment payments. The size of each installment (dollar amount), when it is due (monthly, quarterly, or other fixed period), the length of the installment agreement (two years, 60 months, or other period), and the interest rate applied to installments should be determined with your vender. Other terms may include how much must be paid up front and penalties for prepayments.

▶ **Early payment discounts** —You may be offered a discount as encouragement to pay a net payment early. This may be stated on the invoice as DFI (discount from invoice). If you make an immediate payment, you may save 5 or 10% off the purchase price, as defined in the payment terms.

## Strategies for Extending Payments

No matter how reliable you have been in the past, or how sincerely you promise to pay on time, it's inevitable that your company will eventually experience an unexpected cash flow crunch. Resigning to do nothing is the worst thing that you can do; the best thing that you can do is face this situation head on.

When dollars are limited, you have to prioritize your payments. Of course, tax payments should come first. See that employment taxes are deposited and sales taxes paid on time. Your failure to pay the government can grind your business to a halt. The government can apply a lien to your bank account or even padlock your location until you satisfy your tax bill. What's more, regardless of how your business is organized from a legal standpoint (e.g., corporation, limited liability company), you can be held personally liable for taxes that your business owes.

After paying your taxes, it is highly advisable that you make sure to cover your suppliers and vendors when deciding where to allocate your precious dollars. If you do not, they can cut off the supply of goods you need to stay in business. Also, the suppliers and vendors on your trade accounts may report late or nonpayment to credit bureaus, which would damage your credit rating and adversely impact your ability to raise money in the future.

Instead of making late payments, find other ways to gain more time to pay. Talk frankly with your vendors and suppliers about your problems. If the problems are temporary, the vendors and suppliers may be understanding about an occasional tardy payment.

If you have more serious financial problems that will take greater time to work out, consider some of the following strategies. You could gain more time to pay your bills without damaging your relationship with your vendors and suppliers or hurting your credit rating.

▶ **Forego early payment discounts** — Instead of taking advantage of discounts for paying early, ask your vendor or supplier for additional time to pay. If this is only an occasional request, it shouldn't be a problem. If you find you're asking for added time regularly, recognize that you have a more serious business problem that needs to be addressed and the problem won't be cured with more time to pay a single bill.

▶ **Use materials as security for your payment** — When you purchase materials and supplies, the vendor can hold a lien on them as a way to secure your payment. It is called a *mechanic's lien* or a *materialman's lien*. If you fail to pay, the vendor can take possession of those materials and supplies. Putting a lien on your property is a serious impediment to your credit, so be sure to make timely payments and see that the lien is removed. Removing the lien is not automatic and takes affirmative action on the part of the vendor, but it's up to you to make sure that this is done.

## Seller-Financed Equipment Purchases

If you buy expensive business equipment, such as a radiology machine or a large printing press, it's unlikely you'll pay cash or charge the purchase on a credit card. You'll probably need to finance the purchase. There are various ways to do this.

You can arrange financing through a commercial bank or finance company (this is discussed in Chapter 7). This is common practice for very expensive equipment and sellers often have relationships with finance companies that regularly arrange financing for their products.

In some cases, you can set up a payment plan with the party that sells the equipment. This second financing arrangement is called *seller financing* (the seller does the financing).

Typically, seller financing is arranged as an installment sale. You'll make a down payment followed by monthly payments that include both principal and interest. There is no fixed rule for how sellers must arrange financing, and some may be more flexible or stringent than others. In some cases you may not be required to make a down payment, or you may be able to negotiate for a balloon payment (paying some or all of the principal at the end of the term of the installment contract).

Usually, whether a seller will be willing to extend credit to you and allow you to pay off the purchase price of expensive equipment over time depends on your credit scores (both the owner's and the company's scores). The seller may ask for bank and other trade references in deciding whether you are a good credit risk and can be expected to make payments as required on time.

## UCC-1 Form

The Uniform Commercial Code (UCC) is one of the uniform acts that have been promulgated in an attempt to standardize the laws governing commercial transactions throughout the fifty states. The code is crafted by a uniform law commission but does not come into law unless enacted by the states. The UCC is revised periodically by the commission to bring it in step with modern commercial practices. All of the states have enacted the code at some point in its revisions, but each state may have a different version of the law in effect. For purposes of equipment purchases, the UCC helps to protect the rights of the lender as well as potential future lenders.

Here's how it works. When equipment or other personal (non-real estate) property is used to secure a loan, it is important to protect the lender's rights with respect to the property. Because the property is in the possession of the borrower (debtor), it is necessary to put other potential lenders on alert that the property is not free to be used as collateral for a different loan. This is done by filing a form, which can often be done electronically, with your state. The form becomes a matter of public record for any future lender to see. If the situation is reversed and you become a lender, you can search your borrower's UCC files, which are often accessible over the internet. The form also becomes part of your credit profile.

If you choose to use property to secure a loan, be sure to retain a photocopy of the UCC-1 Financing Statement filed by the lender. The form contains only three vital pieces of information:

▶ The name of the borrower. When the borrower is a sole proprietorship, the owner's name is listed; the DBA is not.

▶ The name of the secured party

▶ A description of the collateral

No signatures are required on the form. In the past, a debtor had to file the form, but this requirement was eliminated several years ago.

## Note:

Most states now use the national UCC-1 form, but your state may have modified it, so be sure to use the one accepted in your location. You can find your state's form at www.iaca. org; www.findlegalforms.com; www.uslegalforms.com; www.uccform.com and www.1stoplegal.com or go to your state's Web site. There may be a fee at certain Web sites for a form download.

Having a UCC-1 form does not preclude you from obtaining additional loans. It is common, in fact, for businesses in certain industries to have multiple UCC-1 forms on file. However, remember that these forms are listed on your credit profile; multiple UCC-1 forms can indicate that you are overextended and are borrowing too much.

## Caution:

Once you have paid off the loan that the property secured, be sure that the lender files Form UCC-3 Termination Form and files it in the same place that the UCC-1 was filed. This shows that you have satisfied your debt and that the property can now be used as collateral for another loan.

# Equipment Leasing

Four-fifths of all U.S. companies, from small businesses to Fortune 500 companies, lease some of their equipment. Leasing is an arrangement in which you essentially "rent" the equipment and machinery your business needs, and can make sense in certain situations. The most common equipment leasing arrangement is an operating lease in which the equipment proprietor (the lessor) leases it to you (the lessee) for use over a set term. An operating lease is also referred to as vendor (or supplier) financing.

Leasing can be used for new or used ("pre-owned") equipment. You may already be familiar with leasing a business car or truck in lieu of buying it. But leasing can be used for just about any type of equipment as well as for certain software.

There are several advantages to leasing rather than buying equipment, including:

▶ **Cash flow** — Leases do not often require a down payment, which is common for equipment purchases. You may, however, have to make one or two lease payments up front (depending on the terms you arrange). Your monthly payment is based on the cost of the equipment and a lease rate factor, which is determined by your credit rating among other factors. Your monthly payment is ultimately the lease rate factor (a decimal number reflecting the rental of the property for the lease term) multiplied by the equipment's cost. For example, if the equipment costs $10,000 and the lease rate factor is 0.0239, the monthly lease payment would be $239. The lease rate factor does not have to be disclosed to you. The monthly cost for leasing equipment is usually lower than what you'd pay to buy the same equipment. There are two reasons for this. First, the lease payments only cover a portion of the equipment's costs, since you are only entitled to use the equipment for the term of the lease. Second, since the lease payments are fixed, you won't have to worry about the escalation of interest rates on credit lines used to finance equipment purchases. What's more, fixed lease payments make budgeting for the term of the loan an easy task.

▶ **Credit preservation** — If you have a line of credit, you can use it for working capital rather than tying up your line paying for equipment.

▶ **Equipment obsolescence** — Some types of equipment, including many technology-related items such as computers and peripherals, may have a relatively short business life. Today businesses replace their computers about every three years; adopting newer and better technology is a necessary measure to keep up with the competition. Leasing gives you more flexibility to replace equipment as technology warrants.

▶ **Tax and accounting considerations** — Lease payments are fully deductible on your taxes and avoid the need to maintain depreciation schedules. Lease payments have no impact on the balance sheet, in contrast to financed purchases which increase liabilities reported on the balance sheet.

▶ **Quick financing arrangements** — Applying for a lease is typically a simpler process than filling out the necessary loan applications for buying equipment. While your credit rating may impact the terms of a lease arrangement, you can usually obtain approval for a lease with less-than-perfect credit. Some credit problems, however, may prevent you from even being able to lease equipment, such as outstanding liens or a bankruptcy within the past ten years. Depending on your credit and the size of the lease, you may obtain approval (or denial) for your application very quickly. For leases of equipment under $50,000, applications for some companies may be finalized within 24 to 48 hours.

Like buying equipment on an installment basis, leasing is a type of financing arrangement in which payments are made over time. You can get a very rough idea of what monthly payments would be on an equipment lease running 24, 36, 48, or 60 months at today's rates by using a leasing calculator (www.advantageleasing.com/calculator.jsp). Of course, the actual payments may differ, depending on your credit rating and other factors.

Leasing can be done directly through the equipment vendor or through a leasing company. A leasing company is a type of finance company that handles leases over a certain amount (usually equipment costing over $5,000). Just as GMAC may handle leases for General Motors cars, you would deal with a leasing company for machinery and equipment you lease. The leasing company may be related to the vendor (e.g., Dell Financial Services for leasing Dell computers) or an unrelated financing company, of which there are many local, regional, and national companies, such as CIT Group for most any type of leasing, or PrimeLease for car leasing only.

Leasing may not necessarily be right for all your equipment needs. Be aware of some drawbacks to leasing:

▶ **Personal guarantee** — You may still have to give your personal guarantee to lease equipment. If the business cannot make the lease payments, you'll have to do so from your personal funds.

▶ **Early termination** — If you want to change equipment before the end of the lease term, you may pay dearly. A lease is a contract and is usually noncancelable for its term. In most cases, you are held to full payment (or substantial early termination penalties) if you want to get out of the lease early. However, in some situations, you may be able to upgrade equipment. For example, if you currently lease a copying machine from a vendor who holds the lease (i.e., there's no third party leasing company involved), you may be able to upgrade to a better machine through the vendor, who can make attractive leasing arrangements for you.

▶ **Maintenance costs** — If the equipment needs repairs or servicing, you may be responsible under the terms of the lease for covering these costs. Warranties for the equipment are held by the vendor or leasing company who owns the equipment, but as a user you may obtain the benefit of the warranties. If you are not protected by the equipment warranty, service contracts can often be purchased and rolled into the lease for maintaining and repairing the equipment. If your locality has personal property taxes, you (and not the lessor) are usually liable for them. The lessor may handle the tax payments with the government, but you ultimately have to pay them.

▶ **Additional purchase costs** — During the term of the lease, the vendor or the leasing company owns the equipment; you only have the right as a lessee to use it. If you decide you want to own the property at the end of the lease term, you have to pay an additional charge. Lease payments do not equate to the purchase of the equipment.

▶ **Removal costs** — At the end of the lease term, the lessee typically bears the cost of returning the equipment to the lessor if it is not purchased.

# Summary

Trade credit from vendors and supplies is one of the most common and easiest forms of credit that a business can obtain. It facilitates the purchase of goods, supplies, and services because businesses don't have to pay vendors and suppliers in full up front.

When equipment is too expensive to purchase with a credit card, you can arrange financing through a commercial lender or finance company, or obtain financing directly from the seller. Paying for expensive equipment on an installment basis can put the needed property into your hands immediately. Nevertheless, the financing arrangement may entail the same formalities (e.g., applications, credit checks) as with commercial financing.

Instead of purchasing equipment or machines needed by the company, consider leasing. Leasing is a type of financing arrangement that allows you to use equipment for a set period. You only pay for the portion of the cost related to the period of use, plus a financing charge. Like a purchase, you may arrange leasing directly with the seller or through a separate leasing company.

Whether you buy or lease equipment, pay careful attention to the terms and obligations of the arrangement.

*"This is what you call vendor credit!?"*

# Did you know?

When looking for vendor relationships, SCORE® advises you to ask your trade association to direct you toward vendors who offer financing arrangements.

# Chapter 7

# Applying for a Commercial Loan

To take a business to the next level, acquire a building, or buy out departing owners, you probably need to borrow funds from a bank or other institutional third party. The Small Business Administration (SBA) announced in June 2004 (the last time these statistics were released) that outstanding small business loans exceeded $522 billion. Each individual small business loan totaled under $1 million, which demonstrates just how common this type of financing is.

Commercial banks fund about half of all small business loans. The other half comes from finance companies, community development corporations, and other sources. The standards banks use to determine whether to approve your loan request can vary considerably from one lender to the next.

This chapter shows you the sources for loans and explains the nature of each of these lenders. It also tells you how loan funds are given to you and how you repay them. Finally, you will learn why obtaining a loan and repaying it on time is vital to your future borrowing.

## Types of Lenders

Loans can come from any number of sources, including yourself and your family and friends. But a standard way to obtain the funds that your business needs (especially if those funds are sizable) is through commercial lenders. (Here, the term "commercial" designates all lenders who are not related to you.) This chapter discusses the following types of commercial lenders:

- ▶ Banks

- ▶ Finance companies

- ▶ Credit card companies

- ▶ Community development corporations

- ▶ Nonprofit organizations

- ▶ Angels

- ▶ Government

## Banks

Banks—such as Wells Fargo, Comerica, and the Bank of New York—offer small business loans of various types. How do banks define a "small business"? The definition varies from one lender to the next. Typically, banks base size on the business's sales volume or revenue. Most of the small business loans offered at the Bank of New York are limited to businesses with revenue up to $1 million. It does, however, have certain loans offered to businesses that make up to $10 million, just as Comerica's small business line of credit is given to companies with a $10 million sales volume.

## Finance Companies

As the name implies, these are companies in the business of lending money. Unlike banks, they do not have accounts where depositors can make money or pay bills; however, they may be willing to lend money to businesses that cannot qualify for bank loans. In exchange for the risk they take, they typically charge higher interest rates and may charge more lending fees.

Many finance companies offer loans akin to traditional commercial financing, but they may also offer alternative financing. Two popular alternative loan options are factoring (based on accounts receivable) and loans based on monthly credit card processing. (Typically a business must have minimum of $3,000 of credit card sales each month for the latter type of borrowing). The upside to finance companies' alternative financing options is that your business credit profile may not be determinative, and a poor credit profile shouldn't affect the acceptance or denial of your loan application. With factoring and credit-card based lending, credit checks are not performed on you or your business. The disadvantage to factoring and credit-based lending is what you pay for this borrowing, which can be very high effective interest rates.

## Credit Card Companies

You have seen in Chapter 6 how credit cards can be used to obtain a business line of credit. Some credit card companies even offer loans separate and apart from their credit cards. Nonetheless, being a cardholder is important to qualifying for the separate loan. Loan options through OPEN from American Express℠ are discussed later in this chapter.

## Certified Development Companies

A certified development company (CDC) is a nonprofit corporation set up to contribute to the economic development of a community by providing loans to small businesses. There are currently about 270 CDCs nationwide. CDC lending is limited to "small businesses" with a net worth under $7.5 million and net profit after taxes under $2.5 million. CDCs that belong to the National Association of Development Companies are listed in the association's directory (www.nadco.org/search_advanced.asp?mode=org).

CDCs are authorized to provide loans through a special program, called a 504 loan program, created by the Small Business Administration. The SBA does not make the loan or even contribute one penny toward it; the CDC sells debentures to the public to raise the money needed for the loan, and the SBA guarantees these debentures. 504 loans are discussed in more detail later in this chapter.

## Nonprofit Organizations

CDCs are just one type of nonprofit organization providing lending assistance to small businesses. Because CDCs only make 504 loans, small businesses may need to look elsewhere for financing under other SBA-loan programs. For example, there are other nonprofit community-based lenders, called *intermediaries,* that are eligible under the SBA to make microloans up to $35,000 (the average loan is $13,000). Funds are available for start-ups and growing businesses, with repayment terms limited to six years and interest rates between 8% and 13%. Intermediaries set their own lending and credit requirements. In most cases, collateral and the owner's guarantee are required. For a list of intermediary microlenders, go to www.sba.gov and enter "microlenders" in the search box.

There are other nonprofit organizations that operate without government support for their lending programs. These organizations provide lending assistance to small businesses. They are sustained by donor contributions and the interest charged on their loans. Because they are charities, they typically have less stringent credit requirements for borrowers.

For example, Count-Me-In (www.count-me-in.org) makes microloans from as little as $500 up to $5,000 for first loans ($10,000 for second loans) to women-owned businesses. The organization claims to be the first online lender with a "unique women-friendly credit scoring system." Another nonprofit organization, Accion (www.accion.org), provides microloans (as little as $100) in the U.S. and around the world to help people get out of poverty by running their own business. Again, credit history may not be determinative. The owner must collateralize some of his assets, such as a car, so that Accion has some security on the loan.

## Angels

As discussed in Chapter 3, angels are investors who provide equity and/or debt financing for small businesses. Typically, loans range from $25,000 to $500,000 (loans over $500,000 are viewed as being in the venture capital arena, which is beyond the scope of this book).

Angels may tread where bankers fear to go, making loans that would not meet commercial lending standards. However, this does not mean that angels toss money around easily. On the contrary, angels are apt to apply considerable scrutiny to your company when deciding whether to make a loan. Usually, this involves careful consideration of your business plan, including all its financial information. They may charge higher interests than a bank if they determine that they are taking a greater risk.

## Government

You may have heard that loans are available to small businesses through the Small Business Administration. This information is wrong. Except in certain disaster situations, the SBA does not make loans directly to small businesses. It does, however, have several loan programs through which it offers guarantees to lenders to encourage them to provide loans to small businesses. (One example of such a program is a 504 loan, described later in this chapter). By providing guarantees that reduce the risk to lenders, there is more incentive to provide money to small companies.

## *Disaster Recovery Loans*

When businesses are damaged by disasters in areas eligible for federal disaster relief, they can apply directly to the SBA for assistance (`www.sba.gov/services/disasterassistance/index.html`). Business physical disaster loans of up to $1.5 million are available to businesses to repair machinery and equipment, to improve leaseholds and fixtures, and to replace inventory not covered by insurance. By law, the maximum interest limit on these loans is 4%. During the disaster recovery period, small businesses can also obtain working capital (economic injury disaster loans) to help pay for necessary and ongoing expenses. Federal loans over set limits ($10,000 for business physical disaster loans; $5,000 for economic injury disaster loans) must be collateralized, and owners must provide their personal guarantee. Repayment for business physical disaster and economic injury disaster loans can run as long as 30 years. The Farm Service Agency (FSA) offers similar loans to farms damaged by disaster (`www.fsa.usda.gov/FSA/webapp?area=home&subject=diap&topic=landing`). Qualifying disaster areas may be found at `www.fema.gov/news/disaster_totals_annual.fema`.

## *States and Local Governments*

State and local governments may offer special loan programs to small businesses as a way to encourage economic development in certain distressed areas. To determine whether any are available in your area, contact your state's economic development agency.

# *Accessing Funds*

Business loans come in all shapes and sizes. The following two options are the principle ways that you can receive the money you borrow:

- ▶ **Lump sum** —The full amount of what you borrow is given to you in one fell swoop, and the principal amount is what the lender agrees to advance to you. Typically, money is either deposited into your business bank account, or you'll receive a check payable to your business. Either way, you control what you do with the money from day one. You use the money by drawing from your bank account. Usually, a lump-sum loan is used to make capital investments, such as purchasing a building or expensive machinery.

- ▶ **Line of credit** — The full amount of what you are authorized to borrow is on account—you may draw upon it when and to the extent that you need it.

You pay interest only on the amount you draw from the account; you will not pay interest on the remainder of the credit line that you haven't used. As you repay the line, you increase the funds available to borrow in the future. Usually, a line of credit is used for working capital.

There are a couple different types of credit lines. For example, there is a *committed line* and an *advised line*. A committed line, which is usually small, is fixed for the promised term—usually one year with annual renewals. An advised line, which is usually larger, is cancelable at any time by either party. With this type of line, the lender monitors the company's activities regularly (e.g., monthly) to see that no problems arise that might affect repayment ability. If the lender notes any activity that he thinks jeopardizes your ability to pay off the loan, the line can be canceled by the bank. Both committed and advised credit lines may be secured or unsecured. An unsecured line is not tied to any collateral; a secured line gives the bank additional security for the loan. Collateral, as discussed in Chapter 3, can be accounts receivable, business assets, or even an owner's personal assets.

## Lump-Sum Loan Programs

When it comes to borrowing, one size does not fit all. Lenders usually offer a variety of lump-sum loan programs to meet the borrowing needs specific to each borrower.

### Microloans

Banks may lend what they view as "small" sums. Depending on the institution, microloans are typically a maximum of $50,000 or $100,000. These loans may be handled internally by different lending officers and may be processed differently than larger loans (lending criteria are discussed below).

### SBA Loans

Lenders, who are called *participants*, may take part in the loan program sponsored by the SBA. Most, but not all commercial banks are participants. The main SBA lending program today is the 7(a) loan program (www.sba.gov/services/financialassistance/7alenderprograms/index.html). The maximum loan under this program is $2 million, of which 75% ($1.5 million) is guaranteed by the SBA (although loans up to $150,000 may have an 85% guarantee). Repayment terms generally run to 25 years, when the funds are used to buy real estate or equipment, and seven years, when the funds are used for working capital. Interest rates on these loans, which may be fixed or variable, are tied to the prime rate. The rate on fixed rate loans of $25,000 or less cannot exceed prime plus 4.25% if the maturity is less than seven years or prime plus 4.75% for longer maturities. The rate on loans between $25,000 and $50,000 cannot exceed prime plus 3.25% if the maturity is less than seven years or prime plus 3.75% for longer maturities. For larger loans, the rate cannot exceed prime plus 2.25% if the maturity is less than seven years or prime plus 2.75% for longer maturities. (Interest rates are subject to change at any time.) These loans have fees and prepayment penalties associated with them.

SBAExpress loans, which can be up to $350,000, are revolving lines of credit that can run for up to seven years. The maximum guaranty by the SBA for these loans is 50%. For more information on SBAExpress loans, go to `www.sba.gov/services/financialassistance/7alenderprograms/sbaexpress/index.html`.

Some commercial lenders also participate in the SBA-sponsored export working capital program (EWCP). According to the SBA, 97% of all U.S. exporters are small businesses. The export working capital program, which is co-sponsored by the Export-Import Bank (another federal agency), provides short-term working capital to small exporters. Together, the SBA and the Export-Import Bank guarantee up to 90% of the loan (`www.sba.gov/services/financialassistance/SpecialPurposeLoans/ewcp/index.html`).

# *Repayment of Funds*

How a loan is repaid can be highly structured or left somewhat to the discretion of the borrower. You may be required to make fixed monthly payments to pay off a lump-sum loan balance over a set period of time. Or you may have the option of paying what you want when you want on a line of credit.

Obviously, interest—the cost you pay for borrowing money—is important in the repayment process. The higher the interest rate, the more motivated you may be to pay off a loan quickly. Assume, for example, that you have a line of credit with a variable interest rate of 15%. If interest rates are rising and you don't pay off the balance, your costs will grow.

It is common practice for commercial lenders to tie repayments to accounts maintained at their banks. For example, Comerica requires a borrower to maintain a checking account from which repayments are automatically debited.

# Commercial Lending Criteria

Understanding how commercial banks decide whether to grant your loan request is helpful to appreciating the value of having business credit. Each lender sets its own criteria, so it's difficult to generalize about exactly what you would face when applying for a loan. However, for purposes of illustration, consider that there are usually two separate criteria: one for microloans and one for larger loans.

Microloans can mean anything from $1,000 up to $100,000. The SBA usually classifies loans up to $100,000 as microloans. Some lenders limit their microloan programs to $50,000. (Larger loans are any loans over the lenders' microloan limits.)

## Microloan Lending Criteria

When it comes to small loans, it's a lot like applying to college. Students submit their SAT scores and GPA, and the school puts these numbers through its formula to select prospective students. Lenders process microloan applications in a similar fashion to admission officers. Businesses must submit two key numbers to the prospective lender: the owner's personal FICO score and the business's credit rating (which is frequently its D&B rating). These two numbers will greatly impact the acceptance or denial of the loan application. The owner's educational background, his great personality, and his banking relationship with the lender, never come into play.

The microlending process is usually an automatic up or down. If the numbers are right, the loan is approved. If the numbers do not meet the bank's criteria, the loan is immediately rejected without further review.

The lender will almost universally require a personal guarantee, regardless of the owner's FICO score or the business's credit rating. This requirement is waived only in unusual circumstances where adequate collateral may be provided as security for the loan (e.g., the loan is used to purchase an expensive machine that can serve as collateral for the loan).

**Note:**

**Failing to meet one lender's criteria does not mean that you can't qualify for a microloan with another lender. That lender may have different standards that you may meet. Shop around and don't become discouraged if you are denied an initial loan request.**

## Larger Loan Lending Criteria

Larger loans involve highly technical and careful evaluation of the business. The Five C's discussed in Chapter 1 are the basis for making loan determinations for substantial borrowing. Usually, a lender will also review a company's business plan to see how it plans to use the money and what the business is all about.

The lender will also run the numbers on the company. This is called a "credit analysis" and is based on the financial examination of the business to determine whether it can afford the loan. The lender's primary concern is being repaid on time and in full. While collateral and personal guarantees can protect a lender against the risk of loss, it is a business hassle, which is best avoided by making smart lending approvals. Usually, larger loans are reserved for companies that have been in business for at least two years, so that they've had time to build up a credit profile.

Here are some key criteria used to assess repayment ability. These are based on historical results (how you've done in the past) and projected results (how you're expected to perform in the future):

▶ **Retained earnings** — A business needs to show profits, and also that these profits are not distributed to owners in full each year but are instead plowed back into the business. Keeping profits in a company is called *retained earnings*, which owners use to grow equity in the business.

*Note:*

**Commercial lenders prefer to see that financial statements have been prepared by accounting firms rather than the company itself. Also, they want assurance that the statements conform to GAAP (generally accepted accounting principals).**

▶ **Debt to equity ratio** — Lenders want to see that a company isn't already overextending by having too much debt on hand. This is determined in part by comparing existing debt to the company's equity (retained earnings). If a company's ratio is one to one (debt is proportionate to equity), most lenders would be very comfortable extending more credit to this business. But when the ratio of debt to equity becomes four to one, or five to one, lenders may be very hesitant to add to this company's debt by lending it more money.

► **Receivables history** — A company must have sufficient incoming funds to be able to make loan payments and repay the loan. This is only possible if the company is receiving payments of what it has sold. A lender will examine the age of a company's receivables. If they are on the books too long (aging receivables), it can mean trouble for the business's cash flow, which can impede loan repayment.

Some lenders have a prejudice against companies within a particular industry (perhaps the lender was burned on a prior loan). This doesn't mean that the borrower has failed the financial lending criteria of lenders in general; it simply means that the borrower must look for another lender. A technology company may have great numbers and still be refused a loan. This could be because that particular bank established a policy against lending money to businesses in the technology industry because of bad experiences with other tech companies.

Even though it is the business that is scrutinized when it applies for larger loans from commercial lenders, that does not mean that the owner is off the hook. When it comes to small and mid-sized companies, lenders continue to look at the financial history of the owner (his/her credit score) and require a personal guarantee in most cases.

Some factors have little or no bearing on a loan determination. For example, whether a business is a corporation, limited liability company, or simply a sole proprietorship is not important. Incorporating a business won't give you a leg up when it comes to applying for money. Of course, doing so may help you run your company more effectively, which would put you in a better position to qualify for a loan.

## Loans from OPEN from American Express<sup>SM</sup>

Instead of obtaining a loan from a bank or finance company, you may qualify for the funds you need through OPEN, a division of American Express geared to small business (www. open.americanexpress.com and click on **Loans and Lines of Credit**). OPEN's loans are promoted as being approved on less stringent terms than traditional commercial financing. OPEN offers two types of loans—*installment loans* and *lines of credit*—neither of which require any collateral.

**Caution:**

**Regardless of the business's credit rating or which type of loan is obtained, all OPEN loans require the personal guarantee of the owner or owners.**

## OPEN's Installment Loans

Consider using an installment loan if you want to renovate your facilities, purchase equipment, or expand your business. Installment loans are lump-sum loans from $15,000 up to $100,000 that you receive in full after your loan is approved. The loan is repaid in installments over 24 or 36 months, which you arrange with American Express. There is a fixed interest rate for the term of the loan. Currently, the rate ranges from 7.99% to 15.99%. The rate you pay depends on the present interest climate and the credit ratings of both the owner and the business (the better credit risk, the lower the rate).

## OPEN's Lines of Credit

Consider setting up a line of credit if you need money to cover ongoing expenses such as payroll, inventory purchases, and cash flow needs from seasonal and/or business fluctuations. With a line of credit, you can draw upon funds, as needed, up to your borrowing limit. Lines start at $10,000 and can run as high as $100,000.

You pay only for the amount you borrow. This is done in one of three ways: you can pay in full each month; you can pay the minimum on the account; or you can pay any amount in between. Interest is not fixed; it can change monthly as interest rates change. Currently, the interest on an OPEN line of credit ranges from prime + 1.99% to prime + 4.99%. As with installment loans, the rate you are charged depends on your credit rating (not on how large your credit line is or how much of the line you use).

You can choose to access your line in one of three ways:

▶ Business checks (no additional charge)

▶ Business Capital Line Card

▶ Electronic funds transfer. For example, you can direct that funds be transferred to your bank account.

**Note:**

Payments for an OPEN installment loan or line of credit can be billed to an American Express Business Charge Card, which can add to your membership rewards points.

## OPEN's Application Process

You can begin the loan process online by completing an application. To be eligible for an installment loan or a line of credit, you must have been in business for at least two years. Also, it's advisable to already be an American Express Business cardmember.

Loans up to $50,000 are granted on the basis of credit scores—both the owner's FICO and the company's score from D&B. This is determined when you provide the required information on the online application, including your federal tax ID (EIN), your American Express card number, and other relevant information.

If you want to apply for an installment loan or line of credit over $50,000, you will need to provide financial documents to supplement the online application. These documents will be used by OPEN to supplement credit scores.

Bear in mind when applying for a loan through OPEN: the business and owner must have a positive net worth and positive net income within the past two years and no bankruptcy filings within the past seven years. No matter how great the business is today, if it fails any of these tests, don't bother applying.

It costs you more than just interest to borrow money. For installment loans, you pay an origination fee of 1% of the loan amount. This is paid at the time of the first monthly payment. There are no further fees for loan maintenance. For lines of credit, there is no origination fee, but you pay $250 each year in which you maintain the line.

# 504 Loans

Often commercial loans available to a small business may not be large enough to meet the needs of a company when it is undertaking a big project. A 504 loan can be used to complement commercial financing to get the project done. Consider the following scenario:

A small business is operating from a building it wants to purchase. A bank would provide 50% of the acquisition cost, becoming the first (senior) lender and having the first lien on the property. A CDC would cover 40% of the cost through a junior lien. The owner would be required to put up the final 10% of the project's price from his or her own funds.

504 loans can only be used to acquire hard assets, such as a building or machinery. The definition of hard assets for 504 loans is very broad, covering not only building and machinery costs but also purchasing land, improving land that has already been purchased (e.g., grading streets), and covering soft costs related to the project (e.g., attorney's fees, architect's fees, appraisal fees, title insurance, environmental reports, and the loan fees for obtaining the 504 loan). The project must also be tied to job creation or retention—typically, one job for every $50,000 of the loan ($100,000 in the case of manufacturing). 504 loans cannot be used for working capital, acquiring inventory, or paying off existing debt.

While this loan program is generous, it is only suitable for the right project. A building must be owner-used. For an existing building, an owner must use 51% of it for the term of the loan. For new construction, the ownership requirement is 60% (of which 20% can be permanently leased out). There is a prepayment penalty for the first 10 years of the loan; the penalty starts at one year's interest rate and declines in increments each year (so the maximum penalty would be the payment equal to one year's interest). For example, if the loan bears a fixed interest rate of 7.5% and the prepayment penalty is triggered in the first year of the loan, a payment equal to 7.5% of the outstanding balance would be due.

## 504 Borrowing Limits

The maximum 504 loan is $1.5 million. This limit, however, can be increased to $2 million when the project relates to certain public policies (e.g., women-owned businesses, rural development, export expansion, minority development, and district revitalization). The limit can even reach $4 million for small manufacturers. With these limits, it is easy to see how a small business can achieve a big goal. Say a minority-owned company wants to acquire a $5 million building. With $2.5 million (50%) through a bank loan, it can use the $2 million (40%) limit under the 504 loan program to swing the purchase. Owners would only have to pony up $500,000 (10%).

## Loan Terms

A 504 loan must be repaid over 10 or 20 years. The interest rate is fixed for the term of the loan (the rate is set when the project closes). The interest on this type of loan is much lower than the interest usually charged on a commercial second loan.

It is important to recognize that even though the loan is secured by a building or other hard asset, the loan program still requires a personal guarantee by any owner with an interest of 20% or more in the company.

# Using Loans to Build Credit

Since you will continue to need money throughout the life of your business, borrowing can be a helpful way to increase the odds of obtaining money in the future. Obtaining a loan is half the equation; paying it back is just as important to your business. It is a tangible demonstration of your company's ability to meet its obligations and keep lenders happy.

## Repayment

You need to repay what you owe and do this on time in order to add positively to the company's credit history. On the flip side, if you fail to make required payments on time, it can negatively impact your company's credit history. As with any late payments, a lender will usually report this to the credit bureau, which can impact your future borrowing ability.

Can you get your personal guarantee removed from the loan while it is being repaid? Probably not. Even if your company has been responsible in making loan payments, lenders are not likely to let go of any of their security, which includes an owner's personal guarantee. But you can always ask.

## Credit Loan Zero Balance

When you use a line of credit, you are usually required to bring the outstanding balance to zero for a set period of time (the time varies with the lender). For example, you may need to pay off whatever you've borrowed and keep a zero balance for one month during the 12-month credit line period. Complying with this requirement usually means you can automatically renew the credit line for another term. It also means that you need sufficient cash flow to carry you through that one-month period.

Carrying a zero balance shows you have met lender requirements—an important thing when you apply for a different loan, whether it is a line of credit through another lender or a lump-sum loan through the current or new lender.

# Summary

Knowing where to turn to when you need to borrow a substantial amount of money is the first step to finding the funds you need.

Recognize that in most cases, the owner's personal guarantee is required for the loan, even if the business has a good credit profile.

Determine what type of loan is best suited for your borrowing needs and how you will repay the money.

Borrowing money can be a way to improve your credit rating so you can command bigger loans on more favorable terms in the future.

# Did you know?

Take another look at the SBA's loan programs. It may be getting easier to obtain SBA-backed financing in coming years because of increased appropriations. Under the federal government's budget for fiscal year 2008, the up front borrower fee under the Section 504 Certified Development Company program would be eliminated, the Microloan program would become self-financing, and the ease of obtaining disaster loans would be facilitated through online applications.

# Working with D&B

Dun & Bradstreet (D&B) is the premier credit rating bureau for businesses. Most companies turn to D&B when deciding whether to do business with other companies. It's where insurance companies look when fixing premiums. And you should work with D&B to establish and maintain credit for your company.

D&B has its roots in a business started in 1841 by Lewis Tappan. His company, the Mercantile Agency, rated customer credit histories for use by retailers and wholesalers. In 1866, Robert Dun took over the business, and within 20 years, the Dun's Book contained information on more than one million businesses. When, in 1933, Dun's business merged with its rival, the Bradstreet (founded in 1849), it officially became Dun & Bradstreet. Today, D&B tracks information on about 70 million businesses in the U.S. and abroad.

This chapter doesn't intend to advertise for D&B. However, because it is the main reporting bureau on business credit, it is essential that business owners understand how to work with D&B as they build their credit proactively.

This chapter explains what a D-U-N-S® number is and how to get one. It covers the D&B program for new companies who hope to gain credibility in the marketplace by creating a D&B credit file.

# D&B Files

D&B keeps track of millions of companies by going through public information and private inquires. When the credit bureau originally started a century and a half ago, information was gathered by credit reporters (D&B claims to have used four presidents—Lincoln, Grant, Cleveland, and McKinley—in this capacity).

Today, D&B files are compiled and maintained by regularly culling through public information. State filings (e.g., when a business incorporates, forms a limited liability company or officially dissolves), court records (e.g., bankruptcies and judgments), newspapers (e.g., reports on business activities), telephone books, interviews with company management, vendors, suppliers, and a host of other avenues act as sources of information for their credit files.

D&B also includes information in their files from companies reporting to it. Large corporations—including banks, insurance companies, utilities, credit card companies, and even the government—routinely report late and delinquent payers. D&B receives accounts concerning more than 639,000,000 payment and banking experiences every year.

Information is continually changing and being updated in D&B files. The company reports that every hour 251 business will have a suit, lien, or judgment filed against them; 246 business telephone numbers will change or be disconnected; 58 companies will change addresses; 41 new businesses will start up; 11 companies will change their names, and seven will file for bankruptcy.

You want to create and maintain a complete and accurate D&B file on your company. This file is the foundation for your company's credit profile. A good business credit profile will not necessarily relieve an owner from his obligation to provide her personal guarantee for third-party loans to the business. It can, however, be helpful in obtaining loans and receiving more favorable repayment terms.

You can supplement the information in your company's file by providing information to D&B, including key management and contact information. You can also supply contact information on your trade accounts. If your vendors and suppliers are also small businesses, they probably do not report credit activities to D&B automatically. It is especially important that you supply information to D&B, so that your file can be amplified. We'll cover this process later in this chapter, in conjunction with CreditBuilder.

# D-U-N-S Number

To facilitate organizing and tracking company information, D&B created a Data Universal Numbering System (D-U-N-S) to assign each business its own unique nine-digit code. Like an individual's Social Security number or a business's federal employer identification number (EIN), the D-U-N-S number can easily identify a company. Sometimes the number appears with hyphenations (Figure 8.1 shows part of a sample D&B report, with a hyphenated D-U-N-S number), but today the D-U-N-S number is commonly written as a straight numerical string. For example, D&B's D-U-N-S number is 150483782.

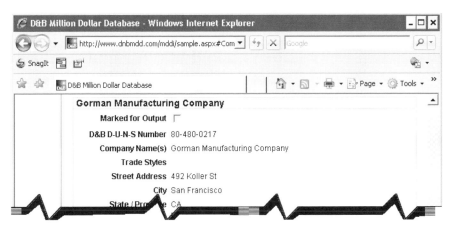

**Figure 8.1:** Portion of a Sample D&B Report with D-U-N-S number (Courtesy of D&B).

The D-U-N-S number was introduced in 1963; today it has gained international recognition. The federal government uses the Data Universal Numbering System in its transactions with businesses. The Office of Budget and Management has required the use of D-U-N-S numbers for all grant applicants as of October 1, 2003. Similarly, all federal contracting opportunities mandate that contractors obtain a D-U-N-S number before registering at the Central Contractor Registration (www.ccr.gov).

The D-U-N-S number is also used by the European Commission (the governing branch of the European Union), the Australian government, and the United Nations in their commercial dealings. Presumably, the D-U-N-S number will gain further usage over time.

The steps necessary to obtain your D-U-N-S number are explained later in this chapter.

## Your D&B File

What does your file look like? The first part of the report on your business contains basic information, including company name, address, telephone number, date the company began , number of employees, SIC number (e.g., 27 41), and your company's line of work (e.g., publishing a newsletter).

Your file also has two key credit-related items: Rating and History.

▶ **Rating** — D&B assigns a rating if it has enough information on your company's credit habits. If it does not have sufficient data, the rating remains blank.

▶ **History** — This can be clear (if there are no known payment problems) or incomplete (if no payment experience has been reported to D&B).

Other sections of your file include:

▶ **Summary analysis** — D&B reports your credit rating or explains the absence of one.

▶ **Payment summary** — This reflects payment information included in D&B files. It shows the total number of entities reporting to D&B, the dollar amounts of the payments to these entities, and what percentage of these amounts have been timely repaid, repaid late, or are still outstanding. For example, if you have paid all of your bills in full within terms, the report shows 100%. The payment summary also lists (as a dollar amount) the highest "Now Owes" and the highest "Past Due" on file, if any.

▶ **Finance** — If you provide financial statements to D&B, this data can be included in your file.

▶ **History** — The legal description of your company is included in your credit file. For example, if you incorporated, a snapshot of state data is included: state of incorporation, type of corporation, filing date, company principals, etc.

▶ **Operation** — This section shows what the company does, such as construction or Web design, as well as the number of employees and facilities.

# Obtaining a D-U-N-S Number

Do you have a D-U-N-S number? Are you sure that you need one? You may already have a number assigned to you; this can easily be checked at the D&B Web site (www. smallbusinessdnb.com).

Whether you need one if you do not yet have one is a separate question. The answer is unequivocally yes. It is the best way to build and maintain your company's credit rating, and it is also required when doing business with certain government agencies, as explained earlier. Moreover, it has been reported that businesses in the Gulf region that already had a D-U-N-S number received federal assistance through the Federal Emergency Management Agency (FEMA) and the SBA's emergency loan programs much more quickly than businesses that did not have a D-U-N-S number. (Chapter 7 discusses SBA's disaster recovery loans and how to apply for them.)

You can easily obtain a free D-U-N-S number just by calling D&B at 800-333-0505 or by registering online at https://eupdate.dnb.com and click on **Get a DUNS number**. If you call, you'll usually receive your number in a matter of minutes; registering online can take up to 30 days. Alternatively, you can obtain a D-U-N-S number through the federal government at no cost in less than 10 minutes by calling 866-705-5711 (the number is required by any company becoming or acting as a federal vendor/contractor). You must provide the following information to D&B in all cases to obtain a DUNS number:

- ► Legal name of the business

- ► Trade name (e.g., "doing business as")

- ► Physical address of the business, including city, state and zip code

- ► Mailing address if different from the physical address

- ► Telephone number

- ► Contact name

- ► SIC Code (the code for the company's line of business)

- ► Number of employees at this location

- ► Headquarters (if different from this location)

You need a separate number for each physical location for your business, as well as for any legal division of a company that may be at the same address ("co-located").

# Getting Rated by D&B

You are no doubt familiar with your personal FICO score, a consumer-based credit rating discussed in Chapter 2. This credit score is maintained by the three main consumer credit rating bureaus—Equifax, Experian, and Transunion. D&B is the preeminent company that provides commercial credit ratings. Their PAYDEX score, which is essentially the business's equivalent to FICO, is assigned to a company with a D-U-N-S number and at least five credit references, which are companies you do business with who can verify your payment history.

The problem for small businesses is the lack of credit references. Small businesses often do business with other small businesses that may not necessarily report to D&B. D&B can help you in this case. It has a product that helps to manufacture (not falsify) a credit file. You need only supply the contact information of businesses you work with, and D&B does the digging on your behalf to build up transaction histories.

## CreditBuilder

If you are a new company or haven't been around too long, you can expedite the process of developing a credit profile by paying D&B for a special service, called CreditBuilder. For $549 or $466.65 with a subscription to other D&B services (a one-time cost), you can start building a credit file immediately and receive a D-U-N-S number in one business day. The total process can take several months, depending on how long your trade accounts take to respond to D&B inquiries.

The file is comprised of at least five credit references. These may include small companies, independent contractors, and sole proprietors, who may not otherwise report to D&B. You provide contact information on your trade references. D&B will contact them and manually add the information they provide to your credit file. By creating the file and populating it with businesses that know you, this immediately establishes credibility for your company.

Here's how it works. You sign up for CreditBuilder online or over the phone. You then provide comprehensive information on your business. Like any good reporter tracking the five W's (who, what, where, when, why), D&B wants to know:

- ▶ Who the business owners are

- ▶ What your company does—its industry, products, and services

- ▶ Where you are located

- ▶ When the company started

- ▶ How the company is organized from a legal perspective (e.g., corporation, limited liability company)

- ▶ Financial statements (this information is optional)

Do you need to go through the time and expense of CreditBuilder? There's no flat answer. It is possible that you choose to build credit passively, allowing the businesses you work with to build your profile as they report about your business. You will build credit references if you do business with major corporations that routinely report to D&B.

However, if you only deal with a handful of large companies, your credit file may remain thin unless you act proactively. CreditBuilder is the only way to add credit references from businesses that would not otherwise report to D&B.

What about companies that advertise that they can help you build company credit? For fees that can cost you hundreds or even thousands of dollars, they promise to coach you in building business credit, but it's unclear whether you get what you pay for. Many of these companies use credit building as a way to advance other services, such as books sales, seminar fees, and incorporation or limited liability company formation (all for an additional fee). In many cases you only learn what you could find out yourself (through this book or directly from D&B). You may wish to stick with D&B products since they are the company that maintains the credit files. This way, you are at least assured that you are doing business with the source.

# *Viewing Your Credit Report*

You can view your report online at any time at www.dnb.com/eupdate. To do so, you need a user name, which is your D-U-N-S number, and a password, which is a six-digit number assigned to you by D&B. To obtain a password, call 800-234-3867.

Once you've logged in, you can print out your report from the screen. Alternatively, for a fee of $29.95, D&B will fax your report to you.

Your report may be very thin and your company unrated if you do not have businesses that automatically report to D&B. Viewing your report may lead you to use CreditBuilder or take other action to create a business credit profile.

Managing your credit report and updating the information present in your report is discussed in the next chapter.

## *Summary*

Invest the time to understand what a D&B file is all about and what information it contains about you.

Obtain a D-U-N-S number to establish business credit as well as to do business with the government.

If you are a new company, take proactive measures to build a credit profile quickly in order to make borrowing easier and less costly.

View your credit report if you have not yet done so in order to verify the information about your company.

*"No, it's okay, that's our DUNS number, not our total debt amount."*

# Advanced Concepts

# Chapter 9

# Monitoring and Protecting Your Credit Profile

Creating a positive credit profile does not mean you can rest on your laurels. You've done the work to establish a positive credit rating for your company. Now, you must continue to be vigilant, guarding your good credit name. Seek out errors in your credit report and get them corrected so you can maintain your good rating.

You should also employ sound business practices that will help you create and maintain a good credit rating. These business practices should be directed toward cash flow management and security protection.

This chapter explains how to review, update, and repair your credit report. It tells you about useful tools that can assist you in this process. This chapter also discusses some common sense business practices to use for maintaining a solid credit profile.

## *Overview of Credit Profile Maintenance*

Putting your best business foot forward is not a one-time activity when it comes to your credit profile; it requires constant attention to detail. The process really entails a two-pronged attack:

▶ Keep a watchful eye on your credit report to ensure that it is accurate. Review your file regularly and take steps when necessary to make changes in your report.

▶ Use sound business practices to avoid credit problems. Monitor your cash flow and bank accounts carefully, so you avoid late payments that can blemish your credit rating. Take appropriate measures to protect your business's bank account and other confidential information from identity thieves. You could become a victim of identity theft and experience credit damage without these security measures.

---

**Note:**

Staying on top of your business credit profile is vital to maintaining good business credit. The same applies to your personal credit. Personal credit maintenance is mandatory for small business owners and should not be overlooked by focusing solely on your business credit.

---

# Reviewing, Updating, and Repairing Your Credit Report

Congress has recognized the importance of giving every consumer the opportunity to review the accuracy of his credit report and fix any problems on it. Toward this end, consumers can review their credit reports for free once every year. Congress has not extended this service to companies, but it shows the importance of credit vigilance.

D&B updates its database every 3.9 seconds. This means that information in your file can change at a moment's notice. You have to be nimble to stay on top of your changing credit report. Remember that businesses that you work with can access your latest information; you want to know when they might find out about any changes in your report.

## Reviewing Your Credit Report

Review your company's credit report on a regular basis to make sure that it is up to date and accurate. Check carefully for any of the following problems that can negatively impact your credit report:

▶ **Old accounts** — Your report may still carry relationships that no longer exist.

▶ **Omissions** — You want your key relationships, such as your largest supplier, to be reflected on your report.

▶ **Identity theft** — Make sure there is nothing on your report resulting from the activities of others that you have not authorized to act on your company's behalf. Just like consumers, businesses can have their bank accounts and personal information usurped by thieves. This can negatively impact your company's credit.

## Updating Information in Your Credit Report

If you detect any problems in your report, take steps to correct them. For example, if your report shows old accounts, get them removed.

If your report fails to include key accounts, get them added. Contact the account or accounts you want added to your report and ask them to report your payment performance to D&B or another business credit bureau.

## Fixing your Credit Report

If you find mistakes in your report, don't assume that they will be corrected on their own over time. It's up to you to see that corrections are made. You do this by contacting the credit bureau.

Put in writing your explanation of what the error is and how it should be corrected. Include in your correspondence your company name, D-U-N-S number, and your personal contact information in case D&B wants to discuss the matter with you. Attach copies of any documents that bolster your position with respect to the error.

Also, if the mistake is the result of a creditor's error in reporting to the credit bureau, contact that creditor and ask for a correction. Suppose a vendor has falsely reported to D&B that you were more than 30 days late in making a payment. In fact, the vendor had extended payment terms to 45 days, and you completed payment within this time. Remind the vendor of the revised payment terms and your timely payment so that the credit report can be corrected.

## Supplementing Your Credit Report

Your report may be accurate but incomplete. You may have additional material that can enhance your credit rating, and it is up to you to bring this information to the attention of the credit bureau. This additional information may include:

▶ **Payroll increases** — If your staff has expanded, let D&B know about this.

Credit bureaus factor company size into a business's credit rating.

► **Financial statements** — On one hand, financial statements of publicly-traded companies are public records that D&B can access to supplement company credit ratings. Small businesses, however, must voluntarily submit their financial statements. Doing so can help D&B gain a better understanding of the financial picture of your company. This is something you would certainly want to do if the financial information is favorable to your company.

## Credit Monitoring

Checking your credit history and correcting errors is not a one-time endeavor. Continually keep tabs on your credit profile to detect problems as they arise and immediately nip them in the bud.

D&B offers a tool called SelfMonitor to help you monitor your D&B credit file (http://smallbusiness.dnb.com/manage-business-credit/Monitor-Business-Credit. asp?cmeid=IOS200430). You can receive e-mail alerts to changes in your file. For example, when D&B changes your PAYDEX score, you receive an alert directing you to view your file and see the change. The cost for this service is $349 a year. Once you receive an alert, you can view your file and make changes, where applicable, at no cost through D&B's eUpdate (http://smallbusiness.dnb.com/manage-business-credit/eupdate-detail.asp).

## Business Practices to Maintain Creditworthiness

You should put into place business practices and procedures that help you maintain or improve your credit rating. It goes without saying that you want to grow your business to improve your retained earnings—who doesn't? But while you are doing this, you can use safeguards to ensure that you don't get into financial trouble and impair your credit rating. This includes cash flow management, banking safeguards, and anti-identity theft measures.

# Cash Flow Planning

Having sufficient money on hand to pay your bills as they come due depends primarily on cash flow. As the word implies, "flow" means that your money continually ebbs in and flows out each month. What's important is that the inflow is there when you need it.

Here are some brief suggestions on how to stay on top of your cash flow. Naturally, each suggestion is not necessarily easy to put into action; this may take time and considerable attention on your part.

> ### Note:
> It is a good idea to work closely with an accountant to help manage cash flow. Use an accountant who is willing to devote the time to this action and who can be helpful in improving your cash flow management systems.

## Use Cash Flow Software

Monitor your cash flow with the aid of software designed for this purpose. Use cash flow features of accounting software (such as Microsoft's Office Small Business Accounting 2006 or QuickBooks) or separate cash flow accounting software.

## Collect Receivables

If you sell to customers on time, make sure to collect in a timely fashion. The older your receivables become, the less likely it is that you'll collect on them. To keep pace with your cash flow needs, implement smart collection policies, including tracking, calling, and using collection agencies where advisable.

## Avoid Receivables by Accepting Credit Cards

Instead of chasing customers for payments, receive them up front via credit cards or other immediate payment methods (e.g., checks, money orders, and PayPal). If you do not currently accept credit cards, obtain merchant authorization through your bank or a credit card processor so you can do so. While there is a cost for accepting credit cards, it avoids the time and hassle of collections.

### Adjust Your Prices

Small businesses are often afraid to raise the price of their goods or services, but you may be out of step with the marketplace. For example, if energy prices are putting a crimp in your budget, consider passing along the added cost by raising prices to your customers. Raising your prices may be a savvy move to ensure adequate cash flow.

### Be Choosy About Your Customers

One important way to protect cash flow is to only do business with customers who will pay you. Unless you receive cash up front, you may be relying on customers' creditworthiness for payment. Depending on your industry, you may want to utilize a monitoring service that alerts you to potential problems with customers. For example, D&B's Customer Watch lets you monitor customers' financial conditions and/or operational status with respect to any D&B reports you've obtained during the past year. You receive alerts (in orange) and severe alerts (in red) to help you make decisions on how to handle these customers, so you can protect yourself against defaults and delinquencies. D&B isn't the only company offering credit reports on businesses. For example, Credit.net (www.credit.net) provides reports on over 14 million companies. Experian (http://www.experian.com/b2b/?hs99=1954) also offers monitoring services on 18 million companies and sends you weekly e-mail alerts.

### Cut Your Expenses

If too much money is going out the door, improve your cash flow by trimming your expenses. Review every expenditure you make regularly to see where cuts can be made. Nothing is sacred, from the magazine subscriptions for your reception area to the expensive lease on a company car.

### Talk with Your Creditors

If you are having trouble paying your bills on time because of cash flow issues, obtain relief by asking your creditors for payment extensions. For example, instead of net 10 days, ask for net 45 days to gain another month of time to pay. You may be turned down, but the request could be granted if it is due to a temporary or occasional need.

## Bank Account Safeguards

Your bank account and how you manage it are prime factors in determining your credit rating. Bounced checks and insufficient funds to pay bills when they fall due can be detrimental to a good credit rating. Overdraft protection and account alert are two ways to protect your company's credit.

## Overdraft Protection

If you operate on a very thin bank margin, you may want to put security measures into place for moments of error. Overdraft protection is a line of credit added to your bank account. If a check drawn on the account exceeds your available funds, money from your credit line is used to honor the check. Obtaining overdraft protection isn't automatic, and you must qualify for it like any other type of loan. You'll incur an added expense with this type of business; interest accrues on the money that you borrow from your credit line. But having the overdraft protection can cushion you when you lack the funds necessary to pay bills on time.

## Account Alerts

Sound bookkeeping practices should keep a tight watch over expenditures and you should basically know what you have in your bank account at all times. However, because money is moving in and out rapidly, it's helpful to employ additional alerts on your bank account so that you can avoid problems.

Wells Fargo is one of many banks that offer account alerts to meet your needs. If your account fees jump when your balance falls below a set level, Wells Fargo will send you an e-mail alert you when your balance is dangerously low. Similarly, if you incur certain bills at a set time each month, you can receive an alert if the funds on hand will not be sufficient to pay these bills.

# Identity Theft Protection

Identity theft is a growing problem for businesses. Typically, thieves ransack companies' files to obtain customers' personal information for consumer ID theft. But increasingly, ID thieves are attacking businesses to:

▶ Steal stationery or other company documents in order to obtain or divert products and supplies that the genuine company is billed for.

▶ Use company information to access business bank accounts and use company credit.

Not only can identity theft impair your credit; it can also seriously damage your brand and company's reputation when business data is used for nefarious purposes.

Protect your computer systems, guard your premises, and even safeguard your garbage. These security measures can keep ID thieves from obtaining your banking information and other sensitive data, which they could use to compromise your credit rating. For example: Review your network's security to determine whether additional protections—hardware and/or software—are required. Depending on the nature of your business, you may want to use encrypted e-mail for added protection of information you send. Limit employee access to key business data (e.g., bank account number).

Limit access to your premises after hours so employees or outsiders cannot get at sensitive business information. This can mean giving keys to the office door to only a few (and retrieving keys from employees who leave the company), installing alarm systems and video cameras to monitor the premises, and using security guards where applicable.

Under the Fair and Accurate Credit Transactions Act of 2003, you are required to shred, burn, smash, or wipe all paper and computer files containing personal information derived from a consumer report (e.g., employee background checks). Apply this same destruction policy to guard your company's sensitive information. Shred all outgoing papers that contain the company's proprietary information. This includes anything carrying an employer identification number, bank account number, computer password, or other information that you want to keep secret. Obviously, you want to protect the confidentiality of your customers, clients, and patients. This same protection should extend to your company's information.

For more tips on avoiding business ID theft from the Better Business Bureau, go to www. bbbonline.org/idtheft/business.asp. You can take a fraud ID quiz online (the quiz is a consumer quiz but can be used for a business as well) at www.javelinstrategy.com/ IDSAFETYQUIZ.htm to see how vulnerable your company is now and to obtain suggestions for improvement. You can learn more about this subject in *The Rational Guide To Preventing Identity Theft* by Jerri Ledford, from www.rationalpress.com.

# *Summary*

Consistently monitor your credit report so that you can correct mistakes and take action when problems arise.

Consider using a monitoring service to stay on top of any changes to your credit report.

Implement business practices to safeguard your credit rating, including smart cash flow management, banking strategies, and anti-ID theft measures.

# Did you know?

Beware of security breaches to computers at government agencies, banks, and other large institutions that can jeopardize your business credit. Identity thieves can use company bank accounts and other information to unlawfully access your money and damage your credit rating. Listen to news reports on these breaches so you can pay extra attention to your monthly bank account and credit card statements.

# Chapter 10

# Re-establishing Credit

In business, there's no such thing as a sure thing. Despite the best plans and the greatest effort, events can transpire to undermine the fiscal health of your company. Some events are external, such as weather conditions or a fire. Other events that impact your fiscal health are internal, such as bad pricing decisions or losing a major customer. As a result of these events, you start to pay bills late and your credit profile takes on a negative face. Some companies may fall into such serious financial trouble as to be forced into bankruptcy.

Whatever the business credit problem, there is usually a solution. Your company can be restored to good fiscal health, and its credit can be repaired. Having a negative or poor credit profile does not preclude your company from obtaining credit while it is trying to re-engineer itself—it just means it will cost you more when you do get it.

This chapter explains how to face reality and fix poor credit. It helps you re-orient your thinking to get a grip on what needs to be done. The step-by-step strategies provided can be used to put your company back on sound financial footing and re-establish its credit.

# Impact of Negative Business Events on Your Personal Credit Report

For consumer credit reports, negative information (e.g., a judgment or lien) can remain on your report for seven years from the date of the event and as long as 10 years in the case of bankruptcy. A discharge in bankruptcy does not remove the event and the poor payment history preceding the event from your credit file. After the discharge, the balance on each discharged debt is reported as "zero" and the history of the delinquency continues to be carried on the report.

Sole proprietors are treated as consumers under bankruptcy law—they are not separate and distinct from their company. This means a sole proprietor facing overwhelming business debt has several options when filing for bankruptcy. A business owner may obtain a discharge and a fresh start through Chapter 7 liquidation. Before filing Chapter 7, the owner's business and personal assets are used to pay creditors as much of their claims as possible. Another option, Chapter 13, allows an owner to pay off his debts, in whole or in part, over a period of three to five years. The owner must use both his business and personal future income to satisfy these debts. (Family farmers should file Chapter 12 rather than Chapter 13 bankruptcy, which provides a simplified repayment plan to pay off debt.)

There's nothing you can do that will expedite the removal of negative events. A personal bankruptcy stays on an individual's credit report for 10 years. Only the passage of time can erase or mitigate this negative information from your file.

**Note:**
Criminal convictions remain indefinitely on a credit report. Their impact may be diminished over time, but you cannot remove them.

# Reality of Fixing Credit Problems

There's no way to minimize the impact of serious financial problems, especially bankruptcy, on your company's credit rating. Anyone who checks on your company's credit profile will receive a serious warning or alert, which may lead the other company to decide *not* to do business with you. This, in turn, can further depress your company's financial condition.

Serious financial problems can make it extremely difficult to borrow money. If you do obtain loans, you'll pay higher rates than businesses with sound credit profiles. Serious financial problems can even impede your ability to obtain insurance.

Rest assured: No matter how serious the problem, there is a credit solution if you are committed to staying in business. What you need to recognize is the reality of the situation.

▶ **Myth:** You can fix credit problems instantly. **Reality:** It takes just as long, or even longer, to repair bad credit than to create an initial credit profile.

▶ **Myth:** You can pay someone to re-establish credit for your company. **Reality:** There's no easy fix. Ads promising to permanently and immediately remove bankruptcies, judgments, and liens from a credit history are just plain false. Be prepared for the repair to take a long time and result from your efforts alone.

# Begin to Resolve Financial Problems

The sooner you can put the company on sound financial footing, the sooner you can start to repair your credit rating. Repairing previous damage to your business credit includes dealing with the debt you already have and practicing wise business procedures to avoid similar problems in the future.

## Work with a Business Debt Consultant

If you are in serious trouble and want to avoid bankruptcy but you can't seem to make headway with your creditors, consider working with a business debt consultant. This type of company can work with your creditors to restructure your debts. Like a consumer credit counselor, a business debt consultant can negotiate with your creditors to devise an affordable plan that can keep your company afloat. This can include extending the time for making payments and reducing the outstanding amount owed. If you have arrived at a critical point where you need to hire a business debt consultant or go out of business, the first alternative may be preferable. Don't expect the business debt consultant to arrive at a quick fix, pay off creditors for you, or repair your credit. It took time to get into debt, and based on your ability to repay creditors, it will take time to get out of debt. Nonetheless, this business counseling can mark a turning point to put you on the road to good financial health and sound creditworthiness.

Here's how a business debt consultant (a debt-restructuring firm) works: You provide the consultant with details about your outstanding accounts payable. This amount is verified by your creditors. Then, the consultant creates a plan based on your budget (what you can afford to pay monthly) and how much the creditors are owed. You can include some or all of your creditors in the plan. For example, you may omit a critical supplier from the plan, provided you can pay what you owe this supplier in full when due without including it in the plan.

There are only a handful of business debt restructuring firms nationwide. The leader is Corporate Turnaround (www.CorporateTurnaround.com). The cost of the service is wrapped into the plan, so you wind up paying back less than you would have if you had paid your creditors in full.

For farmers and ranchers, the U.S. Department of Agriculture provides credit counseling and advice (www.fsa.usda.gov/pas and search for "credit counseling" for access to local offices of the Agency).

Why should you consider using a business debt consultant? There are three key benefits:

▶ **Obtain a break from dealing with creditors** — The business debt consultant takes on the obligation of dealing with creditors, collection agencies, and collection attorneys, so you don't have to do it. This gives you more time to concentrate on running your company.

▶ **Avoid legal fees and bankruptcy** — You can continue to operate your business because costly litigation fees can be avoided. Creditors usually won't force you into bankruptcy if legitimate efforts are being made to satisfy them.

▶ **Start to repair your credit** — Even if you are in the midst of a repayment plan, adhering to the repayment schedule created by the business debt consultant can have a positive effect on your credit profile. It shows you are making payments on time.

## Address Underlying Business Issues

Ask yourself: Why did you get into the financial trouble that impaired your credit? Even if you figure out how to repay existing creditors, you'll only find yourself in the same mess, unless you determine why you got into trouble in the first place. Address these underlying business issues so you can pay your current bills in a timely fashion and avoid similar problems in the future.

Elements that are beyond your control can seriously impact your business. Health concerns of key employees, weather-related catastrophes, fire, and problems with suppliers can impede your ability to complete sales. But usually, businesses get into financial problems because of one main thing—problems managing cash flow. These problems are typically endemic and are caused by conditions that are already present in your company and well within your control. These problems can be boiled down to three main categories:

▶ **Lack of sales** — If you aren't bringing in enough revenue, you won't be able to pay your expenses. By the same token, even if your sales are sound, you may have under priced them and are unable to cover your costs and make the profit you deserve.

▶ **Slow or uncollectible receivables** — Even if you've made adequate sales, your credit may be damaged because you haven't received payments on time or you haven't received your payments in full. This can prevent you from paying your creditors as your bills fall due.

▶ **Undercapitalization** — If you have too much debt, you cannot afford to service it.

Determine which of these reasons, or any other reason, is responsible for your situation and start to address the problem. Like fixing your business credit profile, there's no quick fix for an insidious business problem. You have to recognize the problem, devise strategies for addressing the problem, and then implement the strategies and wait for results.

You may need to turn to outsiders for assistance with your problem. Work closely with your accountant to get a handle on your company's finances. If your accountant is unresponsive, find one who specializes in small companies and is willing to take an interest in yours. Bring in consultants, where useful, to assist you in addressing specific needs. For instance, sales training may be helpful if you determine that your problem is insufficient sales and that your (or your staff's) lack of sales skills is the reason for this problem.

# Affirmative Credit Repair

You can immediately begin to re-establish a positive credit profile. Often, this involves reverting back to the basic credit building practices, which were outlined in Chapter 1. All of the steps used to establish credit are equally relevant to re-establishing it. There's no shortcut to this procedure. The events that negatively impacted your business credit will figure on your credit profile, but if you begin to consistently pay your bills on time, you can reduce the affect of those events on your business's future.

You can also work with your vendors to obtain credit from them or apply for a secured credit card to borrow the money you need to immediately begin repairing your credit history. Both actions will enable you to continue operating your company and to contribute positively to your credit profile.

## Work with Your Vendors

Vendors you have burned in the past may choose not to extend credit to you now. But it never hurts to ask. Hopefully, if you have resolved outstanding problems—by yourself or with the assistance of a business debt consultant—you can regain their confidence in your company. If so, you may be able to obtain *some* credit, making only a partial payment up front. Or you may receive more significant credit, but will be charged for the privilege or face lower limits on advances.

Your best strategy for working with vendors is to employ sound negotiation skills. Remember that vendors want the business and may be amenable to a reasoned request from you. Start out in small steps to show vendors your ability to meet your obligations now, even if you've had problems in the past. Then, build from here.

## Use Secured Credit Cards and Loans

One way to re-establish credit, as described in Chapter 5, is to obtain a secured credit card or a secured loan. The card looks like an unsecured (regular) credit card, so retailers accepting payment do not know that you are using a secured credit card. When you repay the balance on the card, you start to create a positive credit history. The card issuer may also increase your credit line without requiring any additional deposit, making the card only partly secured.

The main value of these cards is the potential for enhancing your credit report. This can only happen if the card issuer reports to D&B and the consumer reporting bureaus where applicable.

> *Note:*
>
> **When shopping around for a secured credit card, ask whether the company reports to D&B. Only accept a card from a company that reports to D&B so you can build your credit rating.**

The Federal Trade Commission warns that many secured credit card offers are scams, so be careful which ones you respond to. Beware of deceptive advertising claims, where the advertiser is not the party offering the cards. Some companies sell the phone numbers of banks offering secured cards; this is information that you can easily search for yourself for free. Some advertisers may use "900" phone numbers (the cost of which can range from $2 to more than $50) or added fees and processing charges to obtain the card. They may even deceptively offer to clean up or repair your credit as part of obtaining the secured credit card, which is something that no amount of money can do.

> *Note:*
>
> **Also consider "poor" credit cards. These are credit cards that do not require any security, but usually have higher annual fees, setup charges, and high annual interest rates. Your credit line on these cards may be very limited. Still, the cards can be useful in showing that you now pay your bills on time. Again, make sure the card issuer reports to the appropriate credit bureaus.**

# Summary

Recognize that repairing debt for a business is not quick or easy. Be prepared to put in the time and effort required to re-establish your company's credit following financial troubles.

Pay off existing debt with the assistance of a debt-restructuring company where applicable. Determine the cause of your company's business problems and address them, taking a long-term approach.

Use a secured credit card to help re-establish a good payment history, but use caution when obtaining this type of credit card.

*"Oh Credit Fairy, please help me!"*

# Chapter 11

# Working with the Government

The federal government spends roughly $350 billion annually to buy goods and services from private companies. Under law, approximately 23%, or $80.5 billion, is supposed to be allocated to small businesses, 7% ($24.5 billion) to small disadvantaged businesses, 5 % ($17.5 billion) to women-owned and minority-owned businesses and 3% ($10.5 billion) to service-disabled veteran owned businesses. State and local governments spend billions more each year to obtain the things they need from the private sector and many set aside a certain percent of their buying for small businesses.

You can profit from government spending if you know how to compete for it. Whether you design office buildings, make Number 2 pencils, or own a corner deli that can provide catering services, the government is a potential customer. There's practically no limit to the type of company that could consider becoming a government contractor.

First, make sure that you qualify for the contract you want. You must have a D-U-N-S number, show creditworthiness and follow government-set rules to demonstrate that you can handle a contract if it is awarded to you.

This chapter does not provide step-by-step instructions to help you navigate the government-contracting process, although you should gain a basic understanding of what's involved. This chapter does discuss the credit standards and other points you need to address before you start to bid on government contracts.

# *Overview of Government Contracting*

Each year, federal, state and local governments spend big money on just about anything you can think of. This market includes: military procurement at the Department of Defense; civilian procurement at such federal departments as the Department of Energy, NASA, and the Government Services Administration (GSA); prime contractors (you can become a subcontractor to a large corporation already acting as a contractor to the government), and state and local governments nationwide.

To become a part of this vast market, you must inform yourself about the bidding process. Women's Biz.gov provides one of the most comprehensive guides on government contracting at their Web site: www.womenbiz.gov/getting_started.html. You don't have to be a woman or a women-owned business to use this resource or its valuable information.

Essentially, contracting is comprised of the following four steps:

1.  **Find the bid leads**— The federal government posts procurement opportunities online and in daily publications (e.g., Commerce Business Daily, CBD Online at http://cbdnet.access.gpo.gov, FedBizOpps, the single point of entry for government procurement opportunities over $25,000 at http://fedbizopps.gov, and subcontracting opportunities at www.sba.gov/GC/indexcontacts-sbsd.html). States and local governments have their own postings for bid opportunities.

2.  **Obtain the bid package** — Once you find opportunities you are interested in bidding on, download the materials.

3.  **Complete the paperwork** — Gather the information you need to submit a bid that has a chance of success. Gather the financial information necessary to make an informed bid that is both realistic to your company and competitive with other bidders.

4.  **Submitting the bid** — Watch for submission deadlines and verify that you've submitted your bid properly. Bids received after the submission deadline are not considered.

These four steps may sound straightforward, but they're not. Each step is complex and your competition is usually great. What's more, even before you start the bidding process, you must get listed and certified. This chapter focuses on these preparatory steps which lead to the bidding process.

# Getting Listed and Certified

To start the bidding process, you must first list your business with the federal government's contracting registry. Following your registration, you can view bids and receive bid packages. While not required, it is also highly advisable to determine whether your company qualifies for special certification. This certification can, in effect, send your company to the head of the bidding line. As discussed earlier, a certain percentage of government contracts must go to certain types of small businesses. By obtaining special certification, a women or minority-owned business can improve its chances of having the winning bid.

## Getting Listed

Getting listed means registering your company at Central Contracting Registration (CCR), which is your business profile. You complete this process online at www.ccr.gov.

To be included in the small business database and to qualify for the 23% of federal spending that has been set aside for small businesses, your company must meet certain standards for your industry group. Small business standards are based on the number of employees and the average annual gross receipts (revenues). For example: In the wholesale industry, small-business designation is limited to companies with no more than 100 employees. In the retail business, "small" designates companies with no more than $6 million in gross receipts for the year. Currently, business size must be stated every five years, but there is a proposal in Congress to require annual reports on business size.

To be able to register, you *must* have a D-U-N-S number. You cannot even start the registration process without it. Chapter 8 explains how to obtain your D-U-N-S number. You may also need a "CAGE" number. The Commercial and Government Entity (CAGE) code is a five-character ID number used extensively within the federal government. If you do not yet have one, you can obtain this when you register your company through CCR. There is no charge for obtaining this number, and the process is handled entirely online.

## Obtaining Certification

Special designation won't help you borrow money on more favorable loan terms than other companies (no special loan programs exist exclusively for certified businesses), but this designation can help you win government contracts. You aren't required to obtain certification, but if certification can give you an edge, why not take it?

Women-owned and small disadvantaged businesses (including minority-owned businesses) are supposed to be awarded a set percentage of all available contracts. There has, however, been considerable political turmoil surrounding cases where it was alleged that contracts that should have gone to small businesses were instead awarded to major corporations through questionable tactics. For example, one small public relations firm in Seattle had initially won an $8 million contract to do work for a federal agency, but lost it in the end to three multi-million dollar companies, J. Walter Thompson, the Bernard Hodes Group and Cass Communications, even though everyone knows these companies aren't "small" or "disadvantaged."

Determine whether you meet the following certification requirements so that you can proceed to obtain this designation.

► **Women-owned businesses** — At least 51% of the company's ownership must be in the hands of one or more women, all of whom are U.S. citizens or legal residents. You must also provide evidence, such as signatures on loans, leases and contracts, that these women control the business. They have to be involved in key management decisions and the hiring and firing of employees. If you think you may qualify, you can obtain certification online through a number of avenues, including the Women's Business Enterprise National Council (www.wbenc.org). The process can take from 60 to 90 days. The National Women's Business Owners Corporation (NWBOC) also offers a national certification program for women-owned businesses as an alternative to the multiple state and local certifications required by many public and private-sector agencies or prime contractors (over 100 private and public agencies accept NWBOC certification) (www.nwboc.org).

► **Small disadvantaged businesses** — To qualify for this certification, a business must be at least 51% owned and controlled by a socially and economically disadvantaged individual or individuals. Those who are African-American, Hispanic-American, Asian-Pacific-American, Subcontinent-Asian American, and Native American are presumed to be disadvantaged (they do not have to prove the disadvantage). Other business owners must show by "the preponderance of the evidence" that they are disadvantaged. This involves demonstrating that you have suffered long term prejudicial treatment, that the prejudice was substantial in nature, and that the situation was beyond your control. You must show at least one objective feature that has contributed to your social disadvantage, such as race, ethnicity, gender, physical handicap, or long-term residence in an environment that isolated you from mainstream America. All individuals seeking designation as a disadvantaged business must have a net worth of less than $750,000 (excluding equity in the business and a principal residence). More information about qualifying for this designation can be found at the SBA (www.sba.gov/sdb/indexaboutsdb.html).

▶ **HUBZone businesses** — Small businesses that maintain a principal office in certain economically-disadvantaged areas and have at least 35% of employees living there can be designated as a HUBZone small business. This entitles you to preferential treatment under the HUBZone Empowerment Contracting Program. For designation details, go through the SBA (https://eweb1.sba.gov/hubzone/internet).

This is not the exclusive list of special designations. For instances, veteran-owned small businesses may qualify more easily for certain contracts.

*Note:*

The certification process can be daunting, so consider working with a knowledgeable consultant who can guide you through the application process.

# Pre-requisites for Contractors

Being the lowest bidder on a government contract does not guarantee you the contract. The government must issue a certificate of competency before a small business can be treated as the winning bidder. (This certification is separate and apart from any designation you might have obtained as a women-owned business or a disadvantaged small business.) The competency certificate is given on the basis of many elements, including: competency, capability, capacity, credit, integrity, perseverance, and tenacity.

If you want to meet certification standards to become a contractor or subcontractor, you must be able to demonstrate quality control, electronic data interchange (EDI), and financial ability.

## Quality Control

The government expects you to show up front that goods or services you provide meet certain industry standards. There's no fixed way to do this. It can be helpful to develop a company manual on quality control that demonstrates that you meet these standards. It can also be helpful to employ a quality control person to oversee a project where applicable.

## Electronic Data Interchange (EDI)

Make sure that you have the technical capacity for government contracting. Today, much of federal contracting is handled electronically, including bidding, purchase orders, and, where applicable, deliveries. For example, all contracts between $2,500 and $100,000 are handled electronically. More information on EDI can be found at the SBA's Web site (http://www.sba.gov/gopher/Ecedi/Info/).

## Financial Ability

Last but certainly not least, your credit worthiness is critical to securing government contracts. Why? To become a provider, you must have the resources to see the project through on your own. The government will not:

▶ **Prepay for work to be performed or goods to be delivered** — In some cases, you may be able to arrange for partial payment, such as progress payments, as phases of a job are completed.

▶ **Finance your obligation** — If you need cash to purchase supplies or pay your workers, it's up to you to find the money.

The government's micropurchases (those up to $2,500) are handled entirely by credit card. In 2001, which was the most recent year for these statistics, the federal government spent $13.8 billion on credit purchases to 410,000 providers. To be a micropurchase provider, you must accept credit card payments. This capability is indicated on your application (and is also part of bid search databases). If you do not have merchant authorization to process credit cards, you should obtain this to gain from micropurchase procurement.

You also want to become familiar with electronic transfers, which expedite the payment process, because government payment can be made directly to your bank account.

Your accounting systems must comply with contractual obligations. You should be able to produce audit reports, systems controls, and other accounting procedures (e.g., cost accounting standards required by federal acquisition regulations). To obtain payment promptly, you need to submit invoices meeting government standards; your invoices may have to be re-tooled for this purpose.

## Note:

As with most things financial, it is advisable to work closely with your accountant to see that your books are in order and that the contract you are bidding on makes sense for your company. Winning a contract that will lose you money is not a good thing. An accountant can help determine up front whether to bid in the first place.

# Surety Bond Guarantee Program

To obtain a government contract, you may be required to post a bond guaranteeing your performance under the contract. If you fail to perform, the bond's underwriter pays the government for any loss. Small businesses may qualify for special bond assistance from the SBA. Generally, such businesses are contractors and service businesses with average annual receipts for the last three fiscal years of no more than $6 million and that meet other size requirements.

The SBA has a guarantee program designed to assist small businesses that need bonding under government contracts. The SBA can guarantee a qualified surety company up to 90% of any losses incurred under bid, payment or performance bonds on contracts up to $1 million. This makes it easier for a small business to obtain a required surety bond.

An interested small business should apply for a bond through a surety agent who will then submit financial and credit information as well as specific SBA forms to the surety company. The surety company submits all required documentation to SBA for final approval. The SBA charges a fee for this guarantee.

## *Summary*

Understand how government contracting works, including your target market and the bid process.

Get listed on the government contracting registry and, where applicable, obtain special designation for your company to qualify for preferential treatment in government contract awards.

Satisfy prerequisites for contracting awards, including getting your financial house and credit rating in order.

If you need a surety bond for government contracts you may obtain, apply for the SBA bond guarantee program.

*"I knew all we needed was one government contract and we'd be RICH!"*

# Chapter 12

# Running a Credit Check on Others

If your business extends credit to customers, make sure you know who you're dealing with. Just as other businesses check your credit history before extending you credit, you should follow suit and run credit checks on customers you may extend credit to.

You don't want to be in the position of playing catch-up—trying to collect on outstanding receivables by slow or non-paying customers. QuickBooks reports that half of its users experience uncollected debt each year. (In 2000, the estimate for uncollected debt in America was $1.3 billion.) The Commercial Collection Agency Association of the Commercial Law League of America says that the probability of collecting an overdue report is 73% after only three months. The collection probability drops to 57% after six months and just 29% after a year. Since collections are vital to the life of your company, increase your odds of collecting on your transactions by only advancing money and selling on credit to customers that you can expect will pay you. One of the ways to judge your risk when you extend credit to prospective customers is to run a credit check on them.

This chapter explains why it's so important to check a customer's credit history before completing transactions. It explains key times to run checks and how to perform them, including the use of monitoring services.

# *Why Run Credit Checks?*

Miguel de Cervantes's advice "Forewarned, forearmed; to be prepared is half the victory" is relevant to companies that sell on credit and the risks that entails. Getting paid in full in a timely fashion is critical to the financial health of any business. For small companies, it can mean the difference between growing or struggling and surviving or going under. Getting paid on time and in full also avoids the hassles and emotional turmoil involved when customers pay late. After all, what business owner wants to divert precious time to making collection calls? That time could better be used on strategic planning or entertaining prospective customers.

Anyone you choose to extend credit to will certainly promise to pay you, but you need objective factors to help determine whether you can rely on this customer's promise or not. Small businesses often won't run credit checks on customers they extend credit to because of the following three reasons:

- ▶ They may not know they can.

- ▶ They think it costs too much.

- ▶ They don't want to irritate customers by questioning their promises or looking into their credit histories.

None of these reasons are valid, and here's why...

You should know you can check credit history on your customers (you already know they have the right to check on you). It is your right, if not your responsibility, to check the credit history of anyone you extend credit to. The Fair Credit Reporting Act (FCRA) governs individuals' consumer credit reports. This law gives consumers access to their own reports for free and blocks all other individuals from gaining access to these personal credit reports. Only businesses that may extend credit to a consumer or businesses involved in transactions initiated by the consumer may check consumer credit reports.

Doing credit checks isn't too expensive. The cost of checking a customers' credit up front is much lower than the cost of collections, which won't necessarily retrieve your money. Collection agencies charge up to 50% of what it recovers of the outstanding balance, which will leave you with very little of what you thought you'd get paid. A credit report, which can save you this frustration, can cost as little as $15 for basic information to $1,000 for an extensive report (individual reports can be free if you subscribe to a reporting service such as D&B).

Doing credit checks will not adversely affect the customer relationship. A reputable customer will not object to a credit check because he has nothing to hide. Credit checks are a customary business practice and the customer has probably had other checks done on him by other sellers, dealers, and vendors.

Don't let excuses prevent you from applying to your customers the same scrutiny that your vendors and lenders do to you. Make the decision to follow through whenever you extend credit to a customer.

## When to Perform a Credit Check

There are specific times in the course of your customer relationship that you want to check credit. These include:

▶ **Initial determination** — Before deciding to do business with a company or an individual, be sure that this is someone you can rely on for payment.

▶ **Credit limit increase** — If you are considering raising the credit line for one of your customers, make sure the customer can handle the increased responsibility.

▶ **Other situations** — Suppose you read an unfavorable story about your customer in the newspaper. (A company you do business with has experienced a fire or been the victim of embezzlement.) Check to see whether the reported situation impacts your customer's paying ability. A credit check can include judgments, liens, and, most importantly, changing trends in payment history.

Initial determinations can change. Make sure you stay up to date on your customers' status by continually checking up on your customers. Regular monitoring is discussed later in this chapter.

# How to Run a Credit Check

The first step in the credit check process is to have a customer complete a credit application. Obtain key information about the customer to help you determine whether to advance credit. The information you'll need to judge your credit risk is different for businesses and consumers. When dealing with:

▶ **Businesses** — You want to know how long they've been in business, the name of their bank, and their EIN. Also ask for references (e.g., a company's trade account).

▶ **Consumers** — You'll want to obtain information on their major credit cards.

How do you verify that the information provided by the customer is accurate? How do you determine whether the customer is a good credit risk? It is not easy to do this on your own. You'll probably want to use the resources available through a credit bureau. The credit reporting bureau will not tell you whether or not to advance credit based on a credit history, but you can make an informed decision by reviewing the information on a credit report.

Several companies provide credit reports. Select the company that meets your credit-checking needs.

## Reports on Consumers

If you extend credit to your consumer client base by allowing your customers to pay over time or following the transaction, check their creditworthiness before agreeing to do business. For example, if you're a home contractor and allow homeowners to pay you in installments, it's a very good idea to run credit checks on your customer before agreeing to the contract.

You can check credit information at the three main consumer credit reporting bureaus:

▶ **Equifax ePort (www.eport.equifax.com)** — Here you can use a variety of products to help you assess credit risk with your customers. The product you use depends on the number of reports you typically need. For example, if you obtain 15-20 reports monthly, consider a membership ($500). With this you pay $100 per month, plus 3-4 dollars per report.

▶ **Experian (www.experian.com)** — Experian offers a variety of business solution products to check consumer credit, including ScoreRight™ and Credit Profile Report. The cost depends on the service selected.

▶ **Transunion (www.transunion.com)** — Check a customer's credit payment history and verify personal information. Its TransUnion DeskTop provides secure Internet access to all of their reporting services.

## Reports on Businesses

The Fair Credit Reporting Act does not apply to credit reports on businesses. You are free to request a credit report on any business for any reason.

### D&B

Dun & Bradstreet (D&B) has 100 million businesses in its global database. You can access information on a particular company in various ways.

▶ **D&B Small Business Solutions** — You can chose from three levels of reports: the Credit eValuator report for low-risk credit decisions, the Business Information Report for medium-risk credit decisions, and the Comprehensive Insight Plus Report for high-risk credit decisions. With the minimum report, which is free to subscribers, you obtain D&B's assessment of creditworthiness based on past performance. You can pay per report, and the prices are reduced for D&B subscribers. The cost per report to nonsubscribers is $29.99, $99.99, and $139.99 respectively.

▶ **DNBi** — This interactive Web application (http://dnbcreditreport. com/dnbi/) provides important information on a company. It is *not* a credit report, but it helps you verify information from a credit application and gives you other information to make your determination. Pricing is done on a per-customer basis, but there are usually "special pricing offers" available to anyone.

### Experian

This company tracks about 15 million companies. Its SmartBusinessReports™ (www. smartbusinessreports.com) offers small businesses two ways to obtain reports. You can pay on a per-report basis or gain access to unlimited reporting for a monthly fee.

**Note:**

If you need more than five reports each month, it pays to enroll for unlimited reporting. If you often order extensive reports, you can significantly reduce your expense on credit reports with this option.

You can choose from one of four report types, at a cost respectively of 8, 19.95, 39.95 and 44.95 dollars:

▶ **Experian Limited report** — Check key facts about a company (including any judgments) and obtain both a credit summary and a payment summary.

▶ **Experian CreditScore report** — Get everything included in the limited report, as well as information on bankruptcies, tax liens, and a credit ranking score.

▶ **Experian Profile report** — Receive the information contained in the creditscore report as well as payment details, inquiries, and a UCC summary.

▶ **Experian ProfilePlus report** — This report is helpful for checking on public companies because it includes Standard & Poor's information.

## Equifax

Equifax Small Business Enterprise (www.equifax.com/biz/index.shtml) offers credit reports on 22 million small businesses. The report lets you verify business information, determine whether there are any outstanding bankruptcies, judgments or liens on that company, and review a company's existing financial obligations (including bank loans, leases, supplier invoices and utility services). You can also obtain Equifax's Small Business Credit Risk Score™, which helps you make an objective determination about credit risk. To use this service you'll pay a membership fee, plus an additional charge per report.

## Credit.net

Credit.net (www.credit.net) gives you access to over 14 million companies, including 6 million companies with fewer than four employees. A subscription fee entitles you to unlimited credit checks; the cost is $150 a month.

## *Hoover's*

Hoover's (a D&B company) (www.hoovers.com) maintains a database of information on 16 million small to mid-sized companies. If you subscribe, you can search for a company by its name, D-U-N-S number, or more than a dozen other factors. While this database will not provide direct information on credit (i.e., you cannot see a company's payment history), you can use it to verify company sales, number of employees, growth, and other factors upon which you may base a credit decision. The cost varies.

# Monitoring Customers

Early detection of negative payment trends is a prime defense against getting stiffed. Don't expect your customers to tell you about their financial woes; they want to continue enjoying the credit you extend to them. It's up to you to be proactive by continually monitoring your customer.

You may not want to monitor every customer. The decision depends on your financial exposure with respect to each customer.

Just as consumers can subscribe to various services to monitor their personal credit, businesses can use monitoring services to watch their customers' credit. There are a number of credit-monitoring options. Again, distinguish between B2C and B2B monitoring. Two key services for monitoring your business customers are:

▶ **D&B** — Obtain a subscription for credit reports so you can pull information monthly on important customers (see D&B credit report information earlier in this chapter).

▶ **Experian's Business Monitoring** — This service lets you keep tabs on your customers. The cost starts at $25 a month for monitoring up to five companies.

# Summary

Running a credit check on customers you extend credit to is vital to the continued success of your company.

Use credit bureaus to check on your consumer and business customers.

Since a credit profile can easily change, it is important to continually monitor key customers. Run credit checks on them periodically or use a monitoring service.

*"I can assure you dude, my credit is tip-top."*

# Extras

# Glossary

**acceleration clause.** A loan term that gives the lender the right to demand immediate payment or to require additional collateral.

**accounts payable.** Money you owe to creditors (e.g., vendors) for goods and services that you have already received. Also called *open accounts*.

**accounts receivable.** Money that customers and clients owe you for goods and services you have already provided.

**annual percentage rate (APR).** The measure of the cost of borrowing expressed as an annual percentage rate, which factors in interest rates and other charges.

**applicable federal rate (AFR).** A rate fixed monthly by the IRS, which varies by the term of the loan (short, mid, and long-term).

**average daily balance.** A figure that credit card companies use to apply interest and banks use to impose fees or credit interest. For credit cards, the balance is credited on the date a payment is received and debited on the date a charge or cash advance is made or interest is assessed. The daily balances within a billing cycle are totaled and then divided by the number of days in the billing cycle.

**balance sheet.** A financial statement that shows your assets, liabilities, and owner's equity in the company as of a specific date.

**capital.** The amount of money invested in a business.

**capital expenditure.** The purchase of assets, such as equipment, expected to last more than one year.

**cash flow.** The cycle of cash through the business, taking into account money going out and money coming in.

**collateral.** Property held aside as security for the lender.

**compensating balance.** The amount, usually a percentage of the outstanding loan balance, that a lender requires to remain on deposit in a bank account.

**current assets.** Assets, including cash, that can be used in a business's operation within one year.

**current liabilities.** Debts expected to be paid within one year.

**current ratio.** A representation of a company's ability to pay its current liabilities from its current assets. Current assets divided by current liabilities.

**debt ratio.** A representation of a company's debt level. Total liabilities divided by total liabilities plus capital (owner's equity).

**equity.** The owner's interest in the business. For corporations, it is common stock plus retained earnings. See also **capital**.

**factoring.** A type of financing based on accounts receivable.

**finance companies.** Businesses that provide capital to firms; competitors of banks.

**financial statements.** Records portraying a company's financial condition, such as the profit and loss statement, balance sheet, and cash flow statement.

**fixed assets.** Assets not expected to be converted to cash (sold) within one year, such as a building or equipment.

**gross profit.** Revenues before operating expenses. Net sales less the cost of goods sold (for inventory-based businesses) or net sales (for service-based businesses).

**gross profit margin.** A representation of a company's profitability. Gross profit divided by net sales.

**gross income.** See **gross profit**.

**letter of credit.** An arrangement where a lender guarantees your payment to a third party.

**leverage.** Relationship between a company's borrowing and owner's equity.

**line of credit.** A lender's promise to advance funds to a company up to a pre-set limit within a specific time. The line revolves, and more can be borrowed as funds are repaid.

**liquid assets.** Assets that can readily be converted to cash (such as a certificate of deposit).

**liquidity.** A company's ability to convert assets to cash. See also **quick ratio**.

**marketable securities.** Securities that can be readily sold (such as stocks and bonds traded on a public exchange).

**North American Industry Classification System (NAICS).** A system that the government uses to classify businesses.

**net income.** The amount of income remaining after expenses have been paid. See also **profit**.

**net sales.** Sales minus returns and allowances.

**net worth.** The excess of assets over liabilities.

**operating expenses.** The cost of day-to-day business operations.

**operating profit (loss).** Net income or loss before taxes and expenses from transactions apart from the normal course of business.

**operating profit margin.** A representation of a company's profitability before taxes. Operating profit divided by net sales.

**prime rate.** The interest rate that commercial lenders charge the largest corporate borrowers with the very best credit.

**principal.** (1) The unpaid balance of a loan. (2) A primary owner of a business.

**profit.** What an owner hopes to reap from operating a business. See also **net income**.

**profit and loss statement.** A financial statement showing revenues, costs and expenses of a company over a period of time. Also called *income statement.*

***pro forma* financial statement.** A financial statement that includes estimated or hypothetical amounts.

**quick ratio.** A representation of a company's liquidity. Cash, marketable securities, and accounts receivable divided by current liabilities. Also called *acid test ratio.*

**retained earnings.** Net profits accumulated in a corporation after it has paid dividends.

**security agreement.** A type of financing based on tangible assets, such as equipment or machinery.

**seasonal loan.** A loan made for a specific seasonal purpose, such as a loan to fund snow blower inventory before the winter.

**Standard Industrial Classification (SIC).** A system that the government uses for classifying businesses.

**Uniform Commercial Code (UCC).** A law that states use to govern sales and secured transactions; provides standard forms for secured financing transactions.

# Index

# Notes

# Notes

# Also Available From Rational Press...

the **1st** COMPREHENSIVE AND AFFORDABLE **Guide Series!**

FREE Bonus Material at www.rationalpress.com

The Rational Guide To

## Preventing Identity Theft

Jerri Ledford

In this guide you'll learn how to...

- ✓ Build strong defenses to protect your privacy and identity
- ✓ Assess your risk of being targeted by identity thieves
- ✓ Determine whether your identity has been stolen
- ✓ Repair the damage of a stolen identity

ACCURACY ASSURED BY

Patrick Gray

RATIONAL PRESS

Rational Guides for a *Fast-Paced World*™

Patrick Gray
Special Agent FBI, ret.
Director, X-Force Operations
Internet Security Systems

mann
PUBLISHING GROUP

## For a special offer on this book from Rational Press, visit
## www.RationalPress.com/SBCredit/Offer

RATIONAL PRESS

*"Serving American heroes, one business at a time"*

he Northeast Veterans Business Resource Center
s a 501 (c)(3) nonprofit organization. We assist
veteran business owners through all aspects of
the business lifecycle including:

- Start up Assistance
- Business Growth
- Coaching

- Marketing Assistance
- Federal Acquisition
- Teaming

## WELCOME HOME RECENT OIF/OEF VETERANS

www.NEVBRC.org

877.Vet.VBRC (838.8272)
617.938.3933

\* All of our services are at no cost to veterans,
their business partners and spouses.

# IMPORTANT NOTICE
# REGISTER YOUR BOOK

## Bonus Materials

Your book refers to valuable material that complements your learning experience. In order to download these materials you will need to register your book at http://www.rationalpress.com.

This bonus material is available after registration:

► Comparison of Small Business Credit Card Options

► 10 Tips for Building and Maintaining Personal Credit

► Bonus chapter: "Small Business Info for Veterans"

## Registering your book

To register your book follow these 7 easy steps:

1. Go to http://www.rationalpress.com.

2. Create an account and login.

3. Click the **My Books** link.

4. Click the **Register New Book** button.

5. Enter the registration number found on the back of the book (Figure A).

6. Confirm registration and view your new book on the virtual bookshelf.

7. Click the spine of the desired book to view the available downloads and resources for the selected book.

**Figure A:** Back of your book.